STEP-BY-STEP
card making

STEP-BY-STEP
card making

Kate Twelvetrees

Quantum
Books

Contents

Collage and Relief

Printing and Painting

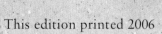

A QUANTUM BOOK

This edition published by Silverdale Books, an imprint of Bookmart Ltd
Blaby Road
Wigston
Leicester
LE18 4SE

Copyright © 1996 Quarto Inc.

This edition printed 2006

This book is produced by Quantum Publishing Ltd.
6 Blundell Street
London N7 9BH

ISBN 1-84573-118-2
QTMGRE

Printed in Singapore by Star Standard Industries Pte Ltd

Papercraft

Fanciful Fabric

Labour of Love

Publisher's Note

The author and publishers have made every effort to ensure that all instructions given in this book are safe and accurate, but they cannot accept liability for any resulting injury, loss or damage to either property or person whether direct or consequential and howsoever arising.

Introduction

CELEBRATING THE CHANGES of the seasons, the festivals which punctuate our year and significant personal events is an important part of our lives. The rise in popularity of purchased hand-made cards reflects our desire to mark these occasions in a special way. Making our own hand-made greetings echoes a time before mass-produced cards were available and every greeting was hand-made. The time, love and work which went into these "keepsake cards" meant that they were treasured – kept in a memento box, inside a book or album, or even framed.

This book offers several approaches to hand-made card making. There are step-by-step instructions describing many different craft techniques in detail, and suggestions of ways in which to use the many different craft tools and kits available. Through these you will be able to experiment with a wide variety of techniques, even if you have no experience of crafts. There are also cards which use other skills, such as dressmaking and embroidery, to make images for cards; and there are many examples of cards which may inspire you to approach card making in the way I do – collecting all kinds of materials and objects from different sources and combining these to make collages. This open-ended approach needs few tools or formal techniques.

It's easy to begin to make your own professional hand-made cards – many people have always made their own Christmas cards – you only need a small amount of space and a few essential pieces of equipment – and you can often adapt what you have. Card making is inexpensive and, because you are working on such a small scale, it is possible to use the best materials which would generally be too costly. I use one exquisite hand-embroidered fabric which costs £125 a metre, a tiny amount makes many cards.

Making your own cards has the added advantage that you can easily give the card a personal significance for the person receiving it – incorporating names, favourite objects and colours, relevant themes, messages and photographs. You will find many examples of ways to do this in this book. Making cards is also a perfect activity to do with children of all ages: it is a means by which they can create an expressive gift for family or friends – they are certainly likely to enjoy this and the results will be cherished. My children, aged three and eight, often come into my studio, gather up little pieces of materials and card and combine these with bits and pieces they have collected in the woods and park to make their own beautifully designed cards.

Look for inspiration for your cards in the gallery sections which show commercial hand-made cards using an astonishing variety of techniques and materials. Use the book as you might use a recipe book,

adapting the lists of materials to what you have available. Think back to other techniques you may have used as a child, or use now in other areas of your life such as plaiting, knotting and even such activities as cooking and carpentry. Look in libraries for books on eighteenth and nineteenth-century craft techniques and adapt these to use in your cards. Experiment, play and, above all, have fun.

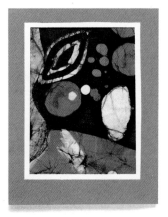

Collecting materials

Once you begin to look around you for materials for your cards you will see possibilities everywhere. Collect everything you can and store things in little boxes, or envelopes until you think of ways in which to use them. Or play with different materials on a card mount and see what images occur. This is an exciting way of working and anything is possible.

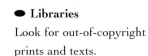

● **From nature** The beach, countryside, city parks and gardens. Shells, feathers, pebbles, seeds, leaves, flowers (pressed, dried or fresh), driftwood.

● **Libraries**
Look for out-of-copyright prints and texts.

● **Around the home**
Pasta, nuts and seeds, dried chillies, aluminium foil, string, wire, buttons, scraps of fabric, furnishing trimmings, broken jewellery, wrapping paper, used stamps.

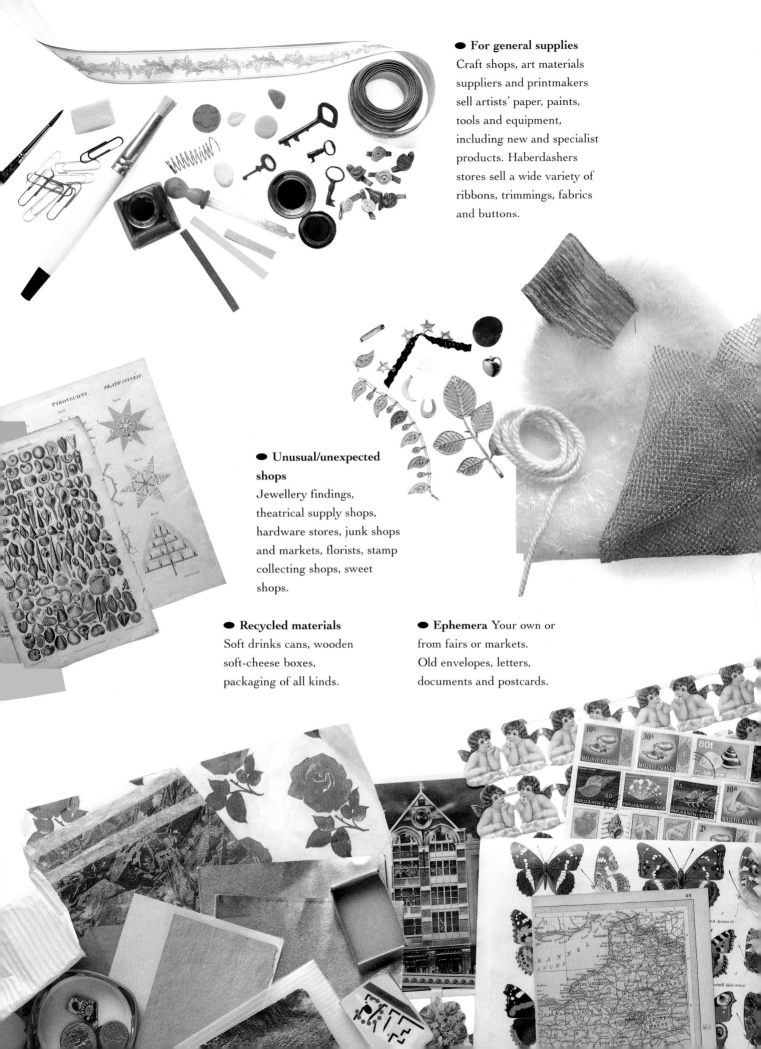

● **For general supplies**
Craft shops, art materials
suppliers and printmakers
sell artists' paper, paints,
tools and equipment,
including new and specialist
products. Haberdashers
stores sell a wide variety of
ribbons, trimmings, fabrics
and buttons.

● **Unusual/unexpected
shops**
Jewellery findings,
theatrical supply shops,
hardware stores, junk shops
and markets, florists, stamp
collecting shops, sweet
shops.

● **Recycled materials**
Soft drinks cans, wooden
soft-cheese boxes,
packaging of all kinds.

● **Ephemera** Your own or
from fairs or markets.
Old envelopes, letters,
documents and postcards.

Basic Equipment

You will only need a few general pieces of equipment. Many of the cards in the book which use a particular craft technique will specify the tools you will need for that individual card.

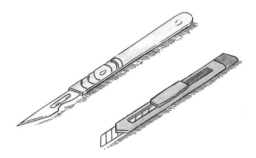

● A good **craft knife**

This is essential – always cut away from your body and with great care. Many professionals use a scalpel instead. However, scalpels are extremely sharp and the greatest care must be taken when using them.

● **A cutting mat**

Card is quite adequate for most purposes, although, unlike a cutting mat, it retains score marks from a knife and so you will need to renew it quite frequently for accuracy.

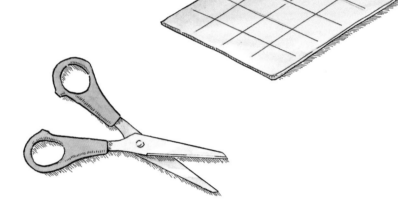

● Sharp **scissors**

Keep the scissors you use for fabric separate from paper or other scissors.

● **A set square**

Especially helpful for cutting accurate right angles. A paper guillotine is very useful, but not essential.

● A metal **ruler**

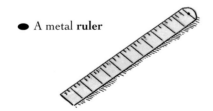

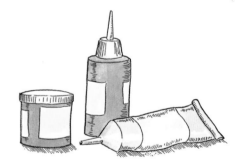

● **Glue**

Three types of glue should cover all your requirements. You will find a reputable fabric/paper glue the most useful. A strong all-purpose adhesive will stick most other materials, and PVA – Marvin medium – dries transparent.

Brushes
Inexpensive artist's brushes in a small, medium and large size are sufficient for most purposes, unless a card requires a more specialist brush.

Iron-on adhesive
This can be used to stick both paper and fabric.

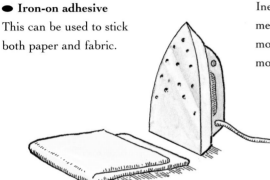

Needles and thread

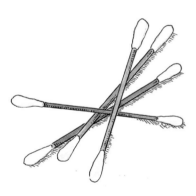

Cotton buds
Very useful for applying glue.

Tape
Sellotape, masking tape, doubled-sided and magic tape are all useful.

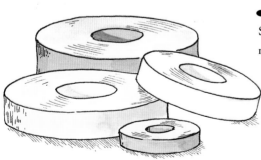

Safety First

Polymer clays (fimo) give off noxious fumes. Always work in a well-ventilated room and, as an additional precaution, do not leave children or pets (including birds) in the kitchen while you are baking clay. The plasticizer in unbaked clays leaches out, so do not store or work with clay in or with utensils and containers that you use for food preparation. As an added precaution, do not use articles made of clay, even when it has been baked, to store or serve food. Always wash your hands thoroughly after you have been working with polymer clay.

~

When cutting sheet metal or wire, such as copper or aluminium, protect your eyes and hands and file all edges smooth.

Basic Techniques

The difference between a professional looking hand-made card and one which just looks home-made is simply the application of a few simple rules. Practising these techniques will be well worth while.

Making a Mount
~

You can buy ready-made cards, with or without windows, but it is very straightforward to make your own.

Cutting and scoring a card mount

1 Use a medium-weight card or a thick paper, such as a watercolour paper. You can deckle edge the paper – see opposite. Cut the card with a craft knife and straight edge to the height you desire and double the width. Use a set square and ruler to ensure the corners are square, and always work on a cutting mat or a piece of thick card.

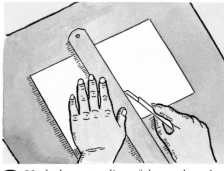

2 Mark the centre line of the card on the outside of the mount with a pencil and lightly score this line with a craft knife, taking care to mark only the top layer of the card or paper with the knife. After completing your card – it is easier to work with the card open and flat – fold the card along the score mark.

Cutting a window mount

1 Using a set square, mark the shape of your window on the card mount with a pencil. Use a ruler to measure from the edge of the card mount to check that the window is centred correctly and not crooked.

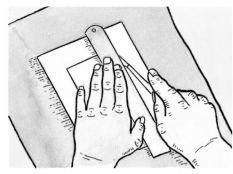

2 Carefully cut out the window using a craft knife and ruler. Be careful not to extend the cuts beyond the corners of the mount. Cut into the mount into and away from the corners for accuracy.

Tracing and transferring an image

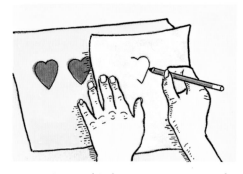

Use tracing or thin layout paper to trace the lines of the picture you wish to transfer. Turn the tracing over and scribble all over the back of the image with a pencil. Turn the tracing the right way up and lay the picture on the mount. Holding the image steady with one hand, go over the lines of the drawing again with a pencil to transfer on to your mount.

For Your Wedding

Masking an image

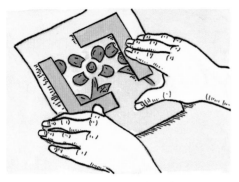

Cut two L-shaped pieces of card, using a set square so that the corners are accurate. Use these to choose the area of a larger print or picture which you would like to frame. By laying them on the picture surface and moving them you can frame any size and shape of the picture. When you are satisfied, mark the area chosen with a pencil mark at the corners and use a ruler and craft knife to cut the shape – don't forget to add on a border to fit under a frame if necessary.

Tearing a deckle edge

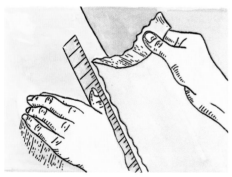

The torn edge which you can find on watercolour and hand-made paper is very attractive. Mark your line with a pencil mark at both margins. Fold the paper over sharply along this line. Use a ruler or kitchen knife pulled through the fold to tear the paper. Do this a little at a time while holding the paper firmly to avoid ripping the paper.

Antiquing paper

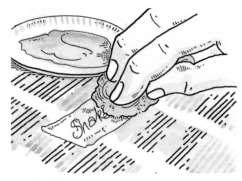

Brush dilute instant coffee over a photocopy of a print. Use a large brush or a sponge and test for colour on a spare piece of paper first as it will dry a darker shade. Don't worry about water marks and different patches of colour, as this will give a better effect. When dry, cut or tear out the pieces you require. If tearing, tear the picture area towards you and away from the background: this will give a stained, rather than a white, edge.

Mounting a print

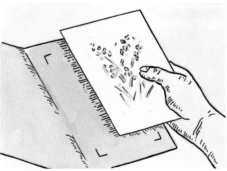

Check that the print is square to the card mount by measuring from the edges (the border). Mark the corners with pencil, so that you can quickly register the glued print.

Basic Guidelines

These are apparently simple rules but it is worth becoming a perfectionist as they can make a dramatic difference to your results. You are not aiming for the uniform look of a mass-produced card, but you do want one which looks crafted and professional.

● Always use a knife with a sharp blade and, if you want a straight line, use a ruler and a good, smooth cutting surface. If you want a right-angle, use a set-square.

● Make sure window mounts are square to your backing mount and always mount images square to their background, unless you are aiming for a deliberately asymmetrical effect.

● Always use a craft knife rather than scissors, when appropriate.

● It is very important to use a good quality card mount of sufficient weight to support the image – this often lets a card down.

● Make sure the score mark is parallel to the mount edges or the card will not fold properly.

● Never let glue be seen on your pictures.

● Always practise new techniques on spare paper first.

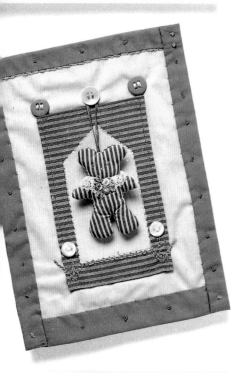

Basic Stitches

~

A number of the cards in this book use stitches as part of their technique. These include straightforward sewing stitches, as well as some simple embroidery stitches.

Slip stitch

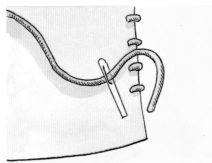

Slip stitches form a neat line of small plain stitches. Bring the thread through to the right side. Insert the needle again to make a stitch and bring it through further along. Continue in this way to form a line of small stitches.

Stab stitch

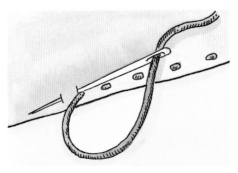

This uses the same technique to make a tiny stitch which is almost invisible on the right side. Stab the needle through the material immediately after the place where you brought the thread through to the right side. Leave a longer gap before bringing the needle through for the next stitch.

Back stitch

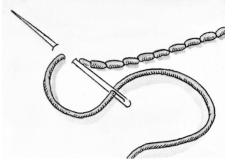

Start with an ordinary stitch and then take the needle back to the end of the previous stitch. Take the point of the needle through to the reverse and bring it through to the right side one stitch ahead. Pull the thread through, then take another backward stitch and proceed in the same way to form a line of joined-up stitches.

Stem stitch

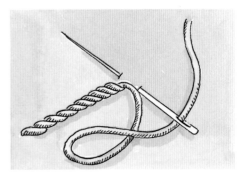

If you are right handed, work from left to right taking small, equal back stitches with the needle inserted from right to left. Keep the thread at the right of the needle. The needle is at a slight angle so that the back stitches overlap slightly as you work. This stitch is often used for flower stems and outlines.

Blanket stitch

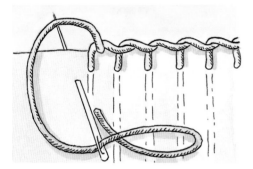

This is worked along the edge of a piece of material. Insert the needle below the edge of the material to the reverse side and so that the needle shows beyond the edge of the material. Loop the thread under the needle and pull it through with the thread below the needle. Space the stitches apart to form a rolled edge.

French knots

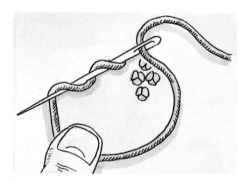

Pull the thread through where you would like to make the French knot. Hold the thread down with the opposite hand and wind the thread twice round the needle.

Tighten the knots and pull the needle back to insert it at the starting point and pull the needle through.

Overstitch on the reverse side to secure, or work another stitch.

Daisy stitch

Commonly used to make leaf and flower shapes, daisy stitch is an isolated chain stitch. Start with a knot on the reverse side and bring the thread through and hold it down with the thumb of your opposite hand.

Reinsert the needle close to where the thread came out, and bring the point out a short distance away so that the thread you are holding loops under the needle point. Pull the thread through gently and fasten the top of the loop with a tiny anchoring stitch.

Gift Wrapping

Wrap your card as you would any gift to make it even more special. Remember to pack and pad your card carefully, if posting it, to avoid damage.

Box

~

METHOD

1 Measure the length and width of your card, add 1cm (½in) and make this your base size, using the template below.

2 Cut out the shape using a craft knife and ruler. Score along fold lines. Apply glue to the front side of the flaps which are shaded in the diagram, and assemble the box, flaps inside.

3 You can cover the box with fabric or patterned paper cut to the same size and stuck in place with iron-on adhesive or fabric/paper glue. Cover the box while flat, before gluing the flaps.

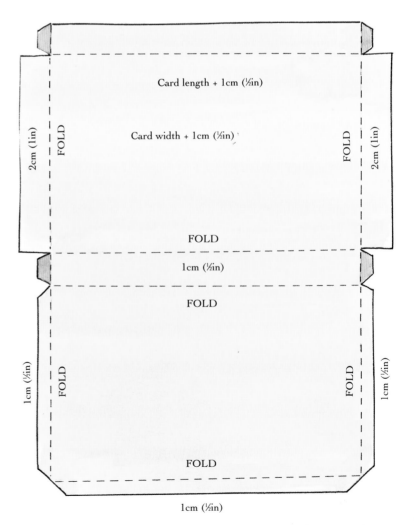

Envelope
~

METHOD

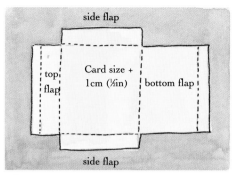

side flap

| top flap | Card size + 1cm (½in) | bottom flap |

side flap

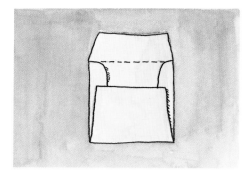

3 Fold in the side flaps, then glue the edges of the bottom flap, turn this up and stick it to the side flaps. Neatly fold over the top flap, then lift it up again and stick double-sided tape below the edge to make a seal.

1 Plan the size of paper required to make the envelope. The basic rectangle should be slightly bigger than the card size. Add a bottom flap three-quarters of the basic width plus 1cm (½in). Add a top flap a quarter of the basic width plus 1cm (½in). Make 3cm (1¼in) side flaps.

MATERIALS

Envelope
~
paper or lightweight card
•
scissors
•
ruler
•
lining paper [optional]
•
paper glue

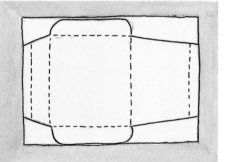

2 Draw the basic shape on to the paper. (You can add a lining paper using coloured or tissue paper the width and length of the envelope minus the bottom flap. Glue it in place before you assemble the envelope.) For a professional finish, use a coin to draw curves on the side flaps. Gently taper the top and bottom flaps.

Wrapping Ideas

● Wrap with tissue and tie with ribbon.

● Buy a card box from a craft shop and cover it with a pretty decorative paper.

● Make a box using a textured or patterned card (see opposite).

● Look for packets of envelopes made from hand-made papers in art shops and good stationers and make your cards to fit them.

● Seal your envelopes with sealing wax and one of the beautiful decorative seals available.

● Make your own envelope using watercolour or textured paper, perhaps with deckle edging (see page 13).

● Decorate the wrapping paper with rubber stamps, stencils or even shells and charms threaded on to your ribbon. The wrapping can reflect the card inside.

Introduction

While it appears one of the simplest of techniques — that of arranging different collected elements into a design — collage/assemblage/relief can be one of the most fascinating and varied methods for card-making. Anything is possible — look around you and you will see possible materials in almost every situation. (We've included lots of suggestions for making a collection on pages 8—9.) The key to successful collage-making is simplicity, an eye for balance and the relationship between materials and colours. Play with combinations of paper, fabric and objects against your background. Don't be afraid to keep changing things around — although the first spontaneous arrangement may be the

Collage and Relief

best. Sometimes I have seen the idea for a

card in the accidental juxtaposition of

materials on my workdesk. Reduce or add until you achieve harmony and balance. Looking at your picture in a mirror can help — the reversed image

gives you a fresh view. The small framework within which you are working means that a few millimetres can make a huge difference but this is a

technique to learn like any other and as you "play" your eye will develop.

Autumn Leaves
~

This mount is made from a very strong, textured watercolour card, and was purchased with a torn deckle edge on one side. It has been cut and scored so that the back of the card is wider than the front, showing the deckle edge. This gives the card a more interesting, layered look when it is closed. Press leaves for the card in a heavy book, between sheets of blotting paper or smooth face tissue, and leave at least one month, until dry and papery.

MATERIALS

Autumn Leaves
~

card mount, 38 × 21cm
(15 × 8¼in), scored to fold as
described above
•
straw paper or other textured
paper, same size as front of mount
•
A4 paper
•
newspaper
•
1 large leaf, such as a fern, either
fresh or pressed
•
selection of leaves, pressed
•
gold acrylic paint
•
rust-red acrylic paint
•
small brush
•
old toothbrush
•
craft knife
•
cutting mat
•
paper glue
•
PVA glue

METHOD

1 Cover the work surface with newspaper. Squeeze some rust-red paint on to a plate. Lay the fern leaf on the *outside back* of the card mount. Mask most of the front of the mount with a piece of paper, except for a strip near the score mark; the card should be open, flat on the work surface. Dip the toothbrush into the paint.

2 Flick the paint on the brush over the leaf with your finger. Do this until all the spaces between the parts of the leaf are spattered with paint.

3 Don't be tempted to lift the leaf to look because you won't be able to get the leaf in exactly the same place again. When you have finished, lift the leaf up very carefully and allow the print to dry.

4 Cut a rectangle of straw paper slightly smaller than the front of the mount. Roughly tear this down the left-hand edge, so that this edge will fall just short of the spatter marks which have overlapped on to the front of the mount. Arrange leaves in a falling pattern on the paper and when you are satisfied with the design, lift them, one by one, and glue down with PVA, taking great care not to break the brittle leaves.

5 Highlight some, but not all, of the leaves by dabbing on gold acrylic paint.

6 Apply a thin layer of paper glue to the back of the straw paper and quickly glue this to the card mount. Glue one small leaf with PVA on the back of the card in the bottom left-hand corner.

Variation
Use a sponge instead of a toothbrush, and press this over the leaf, or mix the two techniques, using two or three leaves and paint colours.

front

back

Christmas Tree Parcels
~

The images on this flat card have been made from a fine webbing used by dressmakers.

METHOD

1 Paint pieces of the vilene with gold and green fabric paint and allow to dry.

2 Make miniature parcels by folding the scraps of card into squares and tying them up with thread.

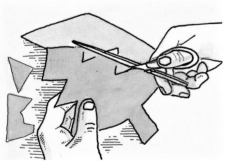

3 Cut a rectangle of gold vilene and a tree shape of green vilene, and glue these in place on the card mount.

4 Tear strips of blue paper and glue to the edges of the mount. Cut out a blue paper pot to hold the tree, and glue in place.

5 Decorate with glitter by applying glue, sprinkling with glitter and shaking off excess. Glue on the parcels and sequins.

Christmas Tree
~

The polymer clay relief combines well with the printed background. A painted modelling clay could be used as an alternative. An old teaspoon was used to make the indentations.

METHOD

1 Roll out the polymer clay. Cut out the tree in green and the pot in brown. Press foliage patterns into the tree, and ridges into pot with the modelling tools. Bake the clay according to the manufacturer's instructions.

2 Fill in the patterning on the tree and pot with glitter glue.

3 Cut a star shape in the flat side of a cut potato by marking the shape with a craft knife and then cutting away the potato around it. Press this shape into fairly thick paint, and use this to print a pattern on to the front of the card mount.

4 Cut a frame to fit the front of the mount from the coloured paper or card. Glue in place.

5 Glue the Christmas tree and pot to th front of the mount.

MATERIALS

Christmas Tree Parcels
~
pale pink card mount, 16 × 16cm
(6¼ × 6¼in)
•
blue paper for border and
scraps of different blue for parcels
•
vilene — stiffening material for
dressmaking
•
gold sequins
•
paintbrush
•
gold and silver thread
•
green and gold fabric paint
•
gold and silver glitter
•
craft knife
•
cutting mat
•
fabric/paper glue

Christmas Tree
~
card mount, 21 × 15cm (8¼ × 6in),
scored to fold in middle
•
thick paper or thin card in
contrasting colour to mount
•
green and brown polymer clay or
modelling clay and paints (see
page 11)
•
acrylic or poster paint
•
glitter glue
•
potato
•
modelling tools
•
craft knife
•
cutting mat
•
PVA glue

Papier Mâché Initial

~

You could choose the favourite colours of the recipient for the initial on this card. The mount is spattered with matching and toning colours.

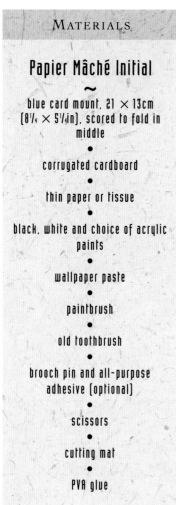

MATERIALS

Papier Mâché Initial

~

blue card mount, 21 × 13cm (8¼ × 5¼in), scored to fold in middle

•

corrugated cardboard

•

thin paper or tissue

•

black, white and choice of acrylic paints

•

wallpaper paste

•

paintbrush

•

old toothbrush

•

brooch pin and all-purpose adhesive (optional)

•

scissors

•

cutting mat

•

PVA glue

METHOD

1 Cut the shape of the initial from corrugated cardboard.

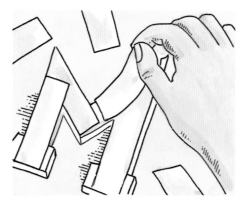

2 Cover with strips of thin paper or tissue, brushed with wallpaper paste. Do about three layers, and allow to dry between each layer.

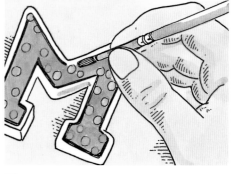

3 When dry, paint white, allow to dry again, then paint a pattern on to the letter.

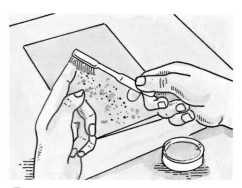

4 Spatter the front of the card mount with paint: apply quite dry paint to a toothbrush and run your finger over the brush, flicking the paint on to the surface.

5 Glue the letter to the mount or fix a brooch pin to the back of the initial with strong adhesive and pin to the card. Self-adhesive brooch pins are also available.

Safety warning
Wear gloves and do not inhale while using wallpaper paste. Try instead to get a non-fungicide craft product, specially for papier mâché, available at craft shops.

Variation
If you have the time, make all the letters of the name. Don't mount them, but make holes through the tops of the letters and string them together.

Floral Brooch
~

This clay takes two days to dry. For a quicker result, use polymer clay (see page 11).

METHOD

1 Cut off a section of clay. Roll or pat flat until it is about 4mm (⅛in) thick and 7 × 7cm (3 × 3in) in dimension. Draw the outline of flowers and vase by scoring the clay lightly.

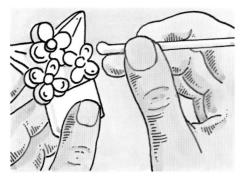

2 Carefully cut out the brooch shape with a clay tool. Make the markings on the flowers and leaves with a moulding tool. Roll three small balls for flower centres and press these flat. Dampen the centres of the flowers gently and press them on.

3 Smooth the whole brooch surface with medium-sized brush or fingers dipped in water, and allow to dry for about two days.

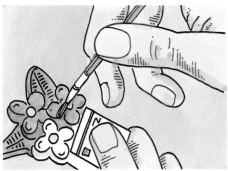

4 When dry, smooth with fine sandpaper, then paint using the fine paintbrush. When the paint is dry, varnish, front and back. Glue on the brooch pin.

5 Cut out one contrasting piece of card and draw a grid of 6mm (¼in) squares for the tablecloth. Cut out the shape of the curtains, glue to the tablecloth, then glue both to the card mount and add details with the other coloured card.

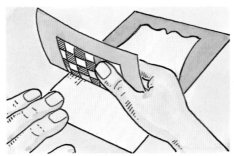

6 Place the finished brooch on the card mount and fix with a loop of wire passed through the brooch pin and twisted inside the mount. On the front of the card, align the brooch with a small piece of blu tack.

Variation

Personalize this professional-looking brooch to suit the recipient(s). You could paint a number 50 in gold for a wedding anniversary, make a pet owner's cat or some vegetables for a gardener.

MATERIALS

Floral Brooch
~
card mount in a light colour,
27 × 16.5cm (10¾ × 6½in), scored
to fold in middle

•

2 smaller darker, contrasting
pieces of card

•

self-hardening clay (DAS)

•

brooch pin

•

gouache or poster paint

•

varnish

•

fine and medium paintbrushes

•

clay tool

•

fine sandpaper

•

10cm (4in) fine wire

•

scissors

•

craft knife

•

cutting mat

•

blu tack

•

all-purpose adhesive

"Wear me" Bracelet

~

The delicate, pastel colours of this card give it a very special quality and it's fun at the same time because the bracelet can be removed and worn.

METHOD

1 Tear out an egg-shaped piece of the decorative paper and wrap a piece of organza ribbon round the base of this to make a basket, gluing the ends of the ribbon to the back of the paper. Glue the paper to the card mount.

2 With a pin, make two pairs of small holes through the card mount, at the top of the egg-shaped paper. Thread two short lengths of wire through these from the inside of the card, make tight loops over the bracelet to suspend it on the card, and thread the wire back inside the card. Secure by twisting the wire.

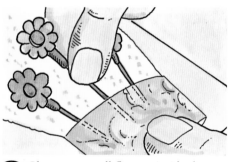

3 Glue some small flowers inside the ribbon basket.

4 You can also write "wear me" on a small scrap of backing paper and glue this at the bottom of the card.

Variation

This also makes a good Easter card. Omit the bracelet, and cut out small pictures of eggs, chicks etc. Glue these to the backing paper above the basket. Alternatively, make a bracelet from sewing elastic and small, wooden alphabet beads, saying "happy birthday" or "good luck".

wear me!

Rose Nest
~

Dried roses are evocative of summer days, parties, wedding bouquets . . . This rose is tucked into a fluffy pink nest of wool.

METHOD

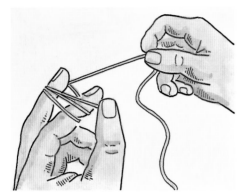

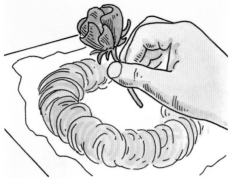

MATERIALS

Rose Nest
~
ivory or cream card mount,
21 × 15cm (8¼ × 6in), scored to
fold in middle

•

small piece of white tissue paper

•

dried rose with short stem

•

angora-style fluffy wool,
approximately 3m (3yd) long

•

fabric/paper glue

1 Hold one end of the wool in the left hand and, with fingers slightly apart, wind the wool loosely around them about 14 times. Remove from fingers and push half of the woollen skein through the hole in the centre to achieve a twisted effect and to stop the wool unravelling. Pass the end of the wool in and out over the ring of wool a few times.

4 Glue the dried rose in the centre, tucking the stem under the wool for extra support. As dried roses are particularly fragile, dot small amounts of glue between the petals on the side of the rose which is being glued to the card.

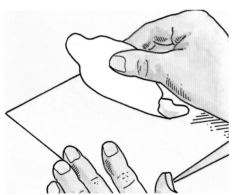

2 Tear an irregular rectangle of tissue, and glue it to the front of the card mount.

3 Glue the woollen "nest" to the mount, making sure that both ends are firmly attached, and that there is no glue on the front of the nest.

Birthday Candles
~

This makes a pretty, tactile card for a child's birthday. Alternatively, for a more sophisticated version to send to an adult, follow the instructions in the variation, below.

MATERIALS

Birthday Candles
~
card mount, 21 × 15cm (8¼ × 6in), scored to fold in middle
•
nursery-patterned ribbon
•
birthday candles (number as child's age)
•
silk flowers
•
scissors
•
fabric/paper glue
•
all-purpose adhesive

METHOD

1 Cut strips of ribbon to fit round the sides of the card mount and glue in place: apply a thin layer of fabric glue to the card, rather than the ribbon, so that it does not stain the ribbon. Glue the bottom ribbon at the ends and bottom edge, to form a pocket.

2 Glue the candles to the card with thin lines of all-purpose adhesive.

3 Put a little fabric/paper glue on the back of the flower stems and tuck inside the ribbon pocket, covering base of candles.

Variation
For a more sophisticated card, simply substitute the nursery ribbon with velvet or lace. Seasonal cards can be made with appropriate silk flowers.

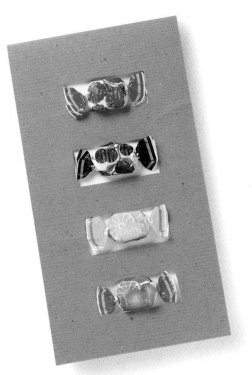

Candies in the Windows

~

Many candies have pretty wrappers suitable for making collages. In this case, whole candies with their wrappers have been glued to the card.

METHOD

1 Cover the front and back of the card mount with brown paper cut to fit: apply a thin layer of paper glue to the mount and press the brown paper on quickly, smoothing it out towards the sides. (The paper looks best with the matt side out.)

2 Place the sweets on the front of the mount and draw box shapes around them. Open the card out and cut these windows out carefully with a sharp craft knife.

3 Close the card and use all-purpose adhesive to glue the candies on to the inside of the mount through their windows to ensure that they are in the right place.

Variation

For a child's card, make a face with candies. Cut out a face-shaped window, and attach two round candies for the eyes, and a rectangular or oval one for the mouth.

River Fish

~

Create interesting effects by photocopying drawings, prints etc. on to clear acetate and layering other papers or fabric behind. The fish-eye rivets hold the acetate to the mount.

METHOD

1 Make a drawing, or use cut-out prints of fish, and arrange and stick the images on to white paper. Photocopy these on to acetate, reducing or enlarging if necessary.

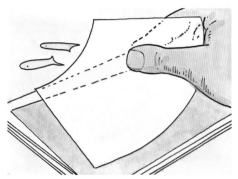

2 Cut acetate to the size of the front of the mount and cut the blue paper and tissue paper into interesting background shapes and layer them on the mount respectively. Hold the acetate on top to check the position. Cut two fish shapes from gold card.

3 Put the two gold fish behind the acetate in two corners of the mount, reposition the acetate and fix all the layers together using the rivet gun, with the rivets as fish eyes.

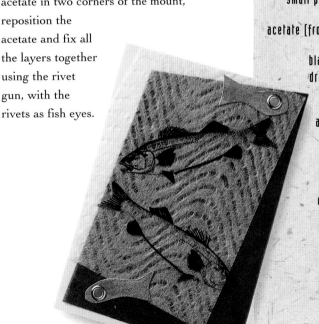

Woven Initial

~

You can use all sorts of natural objects for this card – small shells or pebbles, tiny pieces of glass smoothed by the sea, seeds or even pressed leaves or flower heads. Wood veneer is available from woodwork suppliers.

Woven Initial

~

thick, stiff watercolour paper mount with torn deckle edge, 38 × 22cm (15 × 8³⁄₄in) scored to fold in middle

•

dark blue background paper, slightly smaller than mount

•

sheet of wood veneer, 20 × 10cm (8 × 4in)

•

rope or cord, 90cm (35in) long

•

turquoise acrylic paint

•

pebble

•

cotton wool

•

scissors

•

cutting mat

•

all-purpose adhesive

METHOD

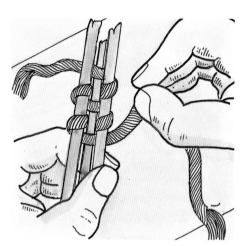

1 Gently break off six narrow strips of wood veneer to make the initial. Hold three strips in one hand and weave the rope or cord through them, weaving the thread back along the next part of the letter with the same piece. If the length of rope runs out halfway through, just leave an extra piece hanging.

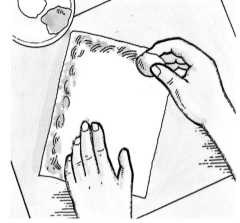

2 Dab paint around the edges of the mount, using cotton wool. Use quite wet paint the first time and then repeat with very dry paint for an illusion of depth.

3 Glue the dark blue paper to the mount and then carefully glue on the initial, making sure that no glue gets onto the front. Glue an extra strip of veneer at the bottom of the initial, to underline it, and add a small pebble to punctuate.

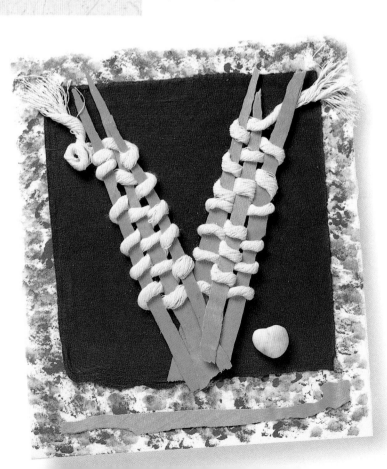

Shells in the Sand
~

It's simple to create your own sand art designs, using double-sided self-adhesive film. Alternatively, use one of the many kits available.

METHOD

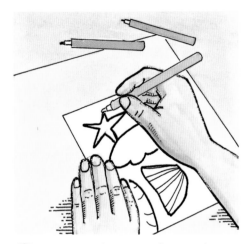

1 Draw your design in colour on the paper, keeping it fairly simple – you will be cutting out each area of colour.

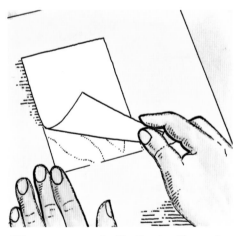

2 Cut a piece of self-adhesive film to the size of your design and transfer your design on to this. Peel the release paper off the back of the film and press the film firmly on to the card mount.

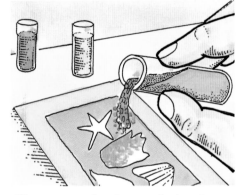

3 Cut around each area of colour in your picture with a craft knife, taking care to cut only through the release paper and not through the film itself. Peel off the darkest area of the design and sprinkle the coloured sand on to this, shaking off excess. Proceed in the same way for each area of the design: you can create interesting effects by mixing the sand colours before sprinkling them on, or by sprinkling one colour very lightly on to the film and a little of another on top.

4 Glue some real shells on to the finished sand picture.

MATERIALS

Shells in the Sand
~
card mount, 21 × 15cm
(8¼ × 6in), scored to fold in
middle
•
sheet of A4 paper
•
double-sided self-adhesive film
•
fine sand in a variety of colours
•
shells
•
coloured pencils
•
craft knife
•
cutting mat
•
all-purpose adhesive

Parcel Postcard
~

Write a simple message or name with sand and stick on a foreign stamp and shells to evoke pleasant memories of travels abroad.

METHOD

1 Write a word with glue on to the postcard-shaped paper: remove the cap directly above where you wish to start writing, as the glue will drip. Quickly and loosely write the word. Sprinkle the sand over the glue, wait a few moments, shake off surplus, and allow to dry.

2 Glue on postage stamp and shells.

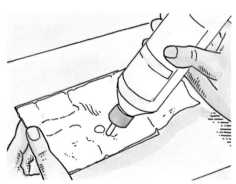

3 Tear strips of tissue and wrap these round the top and bottom of the card, covering only parts of the card. Glue the edges behind the card.

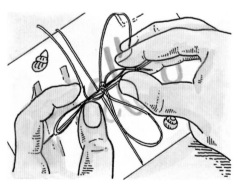

4 Tie the "postcard" with the lurex thread, like a parcel, with long threads hanging from the central bow. Glue the postcard to the card mount.

Embossed Key
~

Use the many powders available to emboss the surface of a rubber stamp. This stamp was copied from an eighteenth-century print, but there is a great variety of purchased stamps available. To make your own stamp see Flying Hearts, page 61.

METHOD

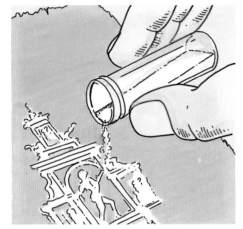

1 Tear a piece of the red paper to fit within the front of the mount. Apply embossing ink evenly to the stamp pad, following the manufacturer's instructions. Print the key on to the paper and sprinkle the print with the embossing powder, shaking off excess.

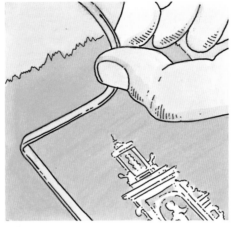

3 Lightly glue the paper to the mount. Glue the ribbon to frame the key, following the instructions given for gluing the ribbon in the Ribbon Frame Card on page 108. Cross the ends of the ribbon at the lower centre edge and glue them to the mount.

MATERIALS

Embossed Key
~

card mount, 21 × 15cm [8¼ × 6in], scored to fold in middle

•

handmade red paper same size as front of card mount

•

narrow gold ribbon

•

embossing ink and stamp pad

•

silver embossing powder

•

key rubber stamp

•

scissors

•

fabric/paper glue

•

heat gun or toaster

2 Hold the printed paper over a heat source, such as a toaster, or use a heat gun to emboss the image. Again, follow the manufacturer's instructions and take care not to brown the paper.

Gallery

1 Seahorse/Saturn
Helen Rowan
Handmade papers, hand tinted with glitter and paint give a rock crystal effect.

2 Holly and Ivy
Kate Twelvetrees
Pressed leaves, hand tinted with gold paint, lie on a velvet background.

3 Colourful Fish
Sands
The fish and the background of this card are cut from two different colours of tissue paper and outlined with 3D paint squeezed on directly from the tube.

4 Love Hearts
Kate Twelvetrees
Candy hearts are wrapped in tissue and tied with silver thread.

5 Sunface/Duck and Dive/Pussy Cat
Irene Baron
Hand-painted paper and papier-mâché can be adapted to a wide variety of images, then mounted on a background of cut-out tissue and patterned papers.

6 FAB
Craig Yamey
A witty collage using international packaging advertising material and sequins.

7 **Lunchtime Pig**

Sparkle Designs
A witty mixed media collage using paper with miniature toys.

8 **Herb Pots**

Personal Stamp Exchange
Five layers of card raise a stamped and embossed image of herbs.

9 **Silver Cow**

Sophie Williams
A kitchen foil cow is machine stitched on to an ink-stained and collaged paper background.

10 **Food Collages**

Tushar Parekh
Two more variations on food collages (see page 37), using glued-on, varnished seeds and chilli wrapped in fine wire.

11 **Red Sails**

Personal Stamp Exchange
Hand-torn tissue paper on a deckle-edged mount forms the background for a detailed embossed rubber stamp image.

12 **Sailing in Brittany**

Crescent Cardboard Co.
A more complex and very delicately coloured version of the sand art technique on page 29.

13 **Heart in Heart**

Irene Brown
A heart made with twisted copper wire frames a cut-out red heart and overlays printed paper and torn tissue.

14 **Ceramic Heart**

Mary Fellows
A hand-painted and varnished ceramic heart is mounted on to two layers of card.

15 **Wedding Card**

Alana Pryce
This unusual wedding card uses an interesting mixture of gold-painted card and lace with a printed definition of the word "marry".

16 **Valentine Hearts**

Personal Stamp Exchange
Layers of embossed and painted stamped hearts are tied on to card mounts with cord or raffia.

Embossed Metal Flower
~

Aluminium sheet is available by the metre from craft/sculptor's supply shops. Alternatively you could use an aluminium drinks can, which is thin enough to cut with scissors.
Take great care not to cut yourself – the edge of the can is extremely sharp.

MATERIALS

Embossed Metal Flower
~

14.5 × 24cm (5¾ × 9½in) card mount, scored to fold in middle
•
inner mount card, cut slightly smaller than card
•
aluminium sheet
•
sequins
•
thin silver wire
•
pin
•
used biro, or similar embossing tool
•
scissors
•
metal file
•
cutting mat
•
sellotape
•
PVA glue

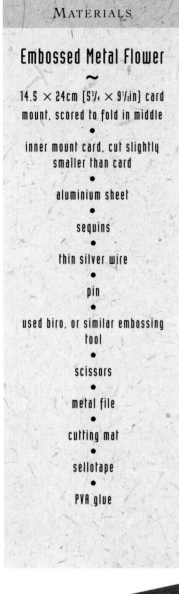

METHOD

1 Cut your design from the aluminium with scissors and file edges smooth. Place the metal on a fairly soft surface, such as several layers of newspaper, and emboss the reverse side with a used biro.

2 Stick the design to the centre of the mount with PVA.

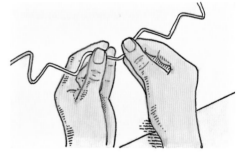

3 Bend the wire into an irregular wavy line – you can do this with your fingers. Using a pin, make two small holes close to each other, near each of the four corners of the mount.

4 Push one end of the wavy wire through one of these holes, fixing it inside the mount with sellotape. Make a border of wire around the card mount, fixing the wire at each corner with small loops of wire passed through the holes. Twist the wire inside the mount to fasten it and then tape it down flat. Finally push the end of the wavy wire through the second small hole and tape down.

5 Glue sequins on the card to decorate. Glue the smaller piece of mount card over the exposed sellotape and wire ends on the inside of the mount.

String Writing
~

This is an easy way to achieve an embossed metal effect. Have fun experimenting with different thicknesses of string, coloured silver paper, and so on.

METHOD

MATERIALS

String Writing
~

coloured card mount, 24 × 17.5cm [9½ × 7in], scored to fold in middle

•

rectangle of coloured paper, slightly smaller than front of mount

•

rectangle of thin card, slightly smaller than paper

•

kitchen foil

•

string

•

dark-coloured acrylic paint

•

fine felt-tip pen

•

paintbrush

•

cotton wool

•

scissors

•

craft knife

•

cutting mat

•

PVA glue

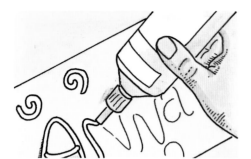

1 Draw the letters of a name on to the thin card. Apply PVA glue along the outlines and leave to become tacky.

2 Lay the string along the lines of glue and trim the end at the end of each letter. Leave to dry.

4 Brush thinned paint over the foil and, before this dries completely, rub most of it off, leaving just enough to create an "antique" texture. (Practise first on a spare piece of foil.)

5 Glue the picture to the coloured paper, and decorate the border with felt-tip pen.

6 Glue the paper to the card mount.

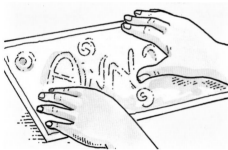

3 Apply PVA glue, thinned with water, to the whole surface of the card. Cover the surface of the card with kitchen foil and smooth this gently over the string, allowing the foil to wrinkle and ensuring that the shapes of the letters are clearly visible through it.

Stamped Parcel
~

Stamped Parcel
~

card mount, 21 × 15cm
[8¼ × 6in], scored to fold in
middle

•

stiff card, 9 × 6cm [3½ × 2½in]

•

coloured paper slightly larger than
stiff card

•

postage stamp

•

buttons, large sequins, jewellery
findings, etc, to thread or tie on
rubber stamp pad

•

thin ribbon or sewing elastic

•

scissors

•

cutting mat

•

fabric/paper glue

Use this basic design to make all kinds of personalized cards. There is a wonderful selection of ready-made rubber stamps available, as well as kits to make your own rubber stamps, and specialist shops which will copy any design in perfect detail. Collect used postage stamps so that you can use one relevant to your theme.

METHOD

1 Apply glue along the edges of the stiff card and lay it, glued side up, on the coloured paper. Fold the edges of the coloured paper over the edges and press down to make a "parcel".

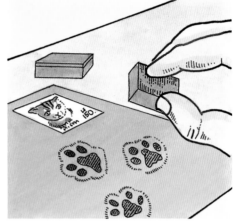

2 Stick a postage stamp to the front of the parcel, and decorate with rubber stamps. You could write a name or short message in the centre.

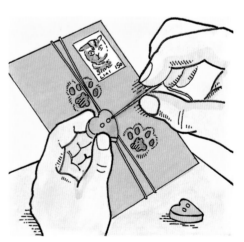

3 Tie the parcel with thin ribbon or sewing elastic, threading on buttons or other motifs, and finally glue the parcel to the card mount.

Variation
Use silver or gold wrapping paper and lurex thread for a Christmas card, decorated with rubber-stamped holly.

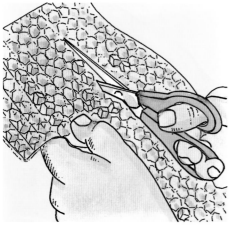

Busy Bees
~

This card uses specially made bee pins on beeswax. They are available from some craft shops and also there are now shops devoted to "bee products", selling honey, beeswax candles and bee memorabilia.

METHOD

1 Cut out a roughly shaped piece of beeswax to cover the centre front of the card, leaving a border all the way around. Position and stick down with all-purpose clear adhesive.

2 When dry, arrange the bees on the beeswax, then push the pin through the beeswax and the card and secure.

Chilli Pepper Collage
~

This witty card uses food motifs with beeswax, combined in a collage of newspaper and tissue paper.

METHOD

1 Cut the beeswax into a small pleasing shape, to fit in one corner of the card. Cut the tissue paper into four rough pieces of different shapes, slightly larger than the beeswax. Cut out a small newspaper cutting of around 7cm (2½in) square.

2 Place the newspaper cutting at an angle in the centre of the card and stick it down with the glue stick.

3 Position layers of tissue paper at different angles over the newspaper cutting and stick each down with the glue stick.

4 When these layers are dry, glue the beeswax on to the top left hand corner of the tissue paper layers with all-purpose clear adhesive. Position and glue the chilli pepper in the same way on the right hand side of the card.

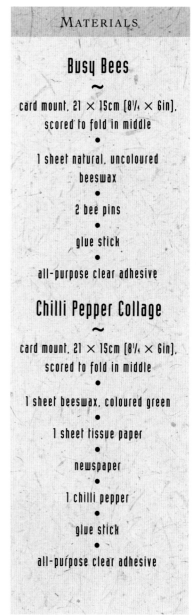

MATERIALS

Busy Bees
~

card mount, 21 × 15cm (8¼ × 6in), scored to fold in middle
•
1 sheet natural, uncoloured beeswax
•
2 bee pins
•
glue stick
•
all-purpose clear adhesive

Chilli Pepper Collage
~

card mount, 21 × 15cm (8¼ × 6in), scored to fold in middle
•
1 sheet beeswax, coloured green
•
1 sheet tissue paper
•
newspaper
•
1 chilli pepper
•
glue stick
•
all-purpose clear adhesive

Hand and Heart
~

Make the heart from an old letter or postcard of your own, or look for something suitable in an antique market or manuscript fair. Alternatively, you could make your own old "manuscript" from paper artificially aged with coffee and marked with a rubber stamp and some fine handwriting.

METHOD

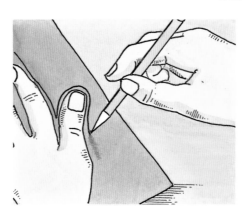

1 Draw lightly around your own hand with a pencil to create a simple outline, then cut it out from the coloured paper. Remove any pencil marks with an eraser.

2 Cut out a heart shape from an old envelope or postcard using the template (see p122), then cut out a second heart from red paper which is approximately 5mm (¼in) larger all round. Stick the envelope or card heart on to the red paper heart, then cut a decorative edge around the paper heart by snipping out small triangular shapes.

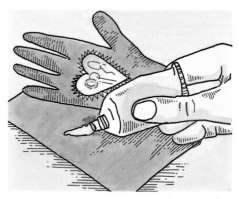

3 Stick the hand on to the card mount, and then glue the heart in to the centre of the palm of the hand.

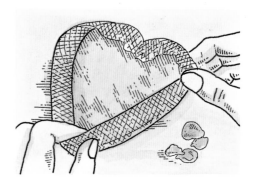

Variation

As an alternative to using a piece of writing, cut the smaller heart from a piece of light-coloured, textured paper, place a little potpourri or dried flower petals on top, and cover with a piece of fine net. Fold the net around the edges of the heart, pleating it as necessary, and glue in place behind the heart. Then complete the card as before.

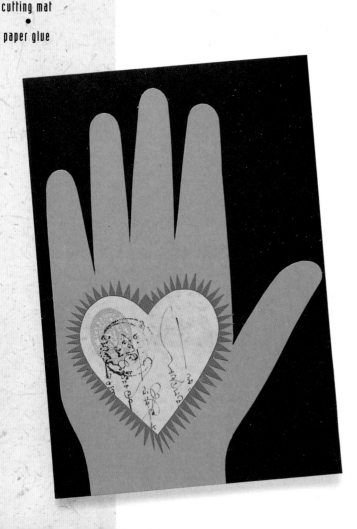

Nostalgic Collage
~

This collage works particularly well because the colours are soft and muted, giving the card an "antique" feel, and the arrangement and careful selection of the objects suggest an old scrapbook or prized collection of ephemera. Press the flowers several weeks in advance as on page 40.

METHOD

1 Cut and tear pieces of old letters, or make your own written fragments using coloured ink and paper.

2 Stick the fragments on to the card mount, leaving room round the edges for the border.

3 Cut out a small motif from the lace and stick on the edge along with the pressed flowers. Sew the buttons to the card in the spaces between, using embroidery thread or raffia. Choose one large flower as a focal point and glue in place. Glue on the photocopied motif(s).

Flower Urn
~

Part of the interest of this card lies in the texture of the paper used for the mount. Instead of the type of paper shown, you could use one which includes fragments of pressed leaves or flowers. For an unusual addition to this card, fix a real packet of flower seeds inside the card.

METHOD

1 Cut out an urn shape from red paper and glue to the bottom of the mount.

2 Cut out small leaf shapes from the green paper and glue them in a tall arch shape above the urn.

3 Starting at the top of the leaf arch, fill in the space with the cut-out flowers and more leaves. Place the smallest flowers at the top to balance the arrangement.

Variation
Try a long, thin back mount with a tall vase of red tulips and long, bright green leaves.

MATERIALS

Nostalgic Collage
~

card mount, 26 × 15cm (10¼ × 6in), scored to fold in middle

•

photocopied engravings (stained with coffee for an antique effect, if desired)

•

old letters

•

pressed flowers

•

scrap of lace

•

small buttons

•

embroidery or raffia thread and needle

•

scissors

•

craft knife

•

cutting mat

•

fabric/paper glue

Flower Urn
~

mount made from thick, light-coloured textured paper, 25 × 25cm (10 × 10in), scored to fold in middle

•

red paper for urn and green paper for leaves

•

photographs or illustrations of flowers cut from old seed catalogues or gardening magazines

•

craft knife

•

cutting mat

•

paper glue

Pressed Flower Wrap
~

To press flowers, simply place them in a heavy book, between sheets of blotting paper or smooth face tissue, and leave for several weeks, then check. Experiment with different flowers, avoiding fleshy ones. The best tissue paper to use for this card is soft, fine tissue, available from art shops.

METHOD

1 Lay the flower on the watercolour paper and mark the paper lightly at the edges of the flower with a pencil. Tear out a piece of the paper to fit around the flower.

2 Lightly glue the flower to the paper, taking care not to break it.

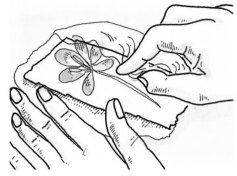

3 Tear out an irregular piece of tissue paper and wrap this around the flower and paper to form a parcel or envelope.

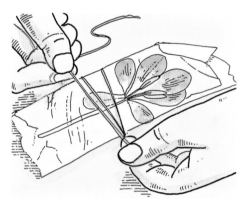

4 Wrap the thread around the parcel two or three times and knot. Pull the thread between thumb and forefinger, in order to corkscrew it.

5 Glue the parcel to the card mount. Be careful not to get any glue on the tissue paper in front.

Feather Card

~

To copy this card, the feather should not be too large, though many variations are possible. Look in parks and on beaches for feathers. They are also available in craft shops but often the prettiest are found ones. When deciding on the writing to go next to the feather, use appropriate wording, such as "with love" or "for you".

METHOD

1 Cut a piece of watercolour paper to suit the size of the feather and trim the edges with decorative-edge scissors. This piece should be smaller than the piece of mottled paper.

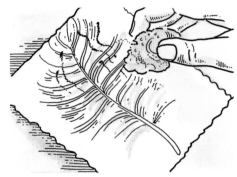

2 Spread glue along the spine of the feather, and press in place on the watercolour paper. Brush, dab or stipple gold paint around the edges of the feather, on the paper and then on to the spine of the feather.

3 Tear out a small scrap of photocopied writing. Stain this with diluted instant coffee to give it an antique effect, and glue on to the paper.

4 Tie the thread round the mounted feather like a parcel, knotting behind, and glue to the mottled paper. Glue to the front of the card mount.

MATERIALS

Feather Card

~

dark blue card mount, 21 × 15cm [8¼ × 6in], scored to fold in middle

●

watercolour paper

●

mottled light blue paper, cut to fit within front of mount, and trimmed along edges with decorative-edge scissors .

●

small piece of handwriting to complement card style, reduced on photocopier

●

feather

●

paintbrush or sponge

●

gold thread

●

gold or other colour paint [powder and acrylic medium]

●

instant coffee

●

craft knife

●

cutting mat

●

decorative-edge scissors

●

fabric/paper glue

Introduction

You can make a print with almost anything — an apple sliced through the centre makes a beautiful image and what more evocative record of babyhood can you make than a tiny hand print in clay or on paper? Another simple method of printing unique images is mono-printing — simply roll oil-based printing ink on to a sheet of glass, draw into the ink with your fingers or the end of a paintbrush, gently press paper on to the ink and lift up your print. A photocopier is one of my favourite "tools". Find a photocopy shop with a good machine which you can operate yourself. You can feed through your own choice of paper — though it must always be cut square and be flat so that it does not block the machine. You

Printing and Painting

can use specially prepared acetate, and reduce or enlarge your images. This chapter also demonstrates some simple techniques such as potato cutting (which can look very professional when used with imagination), lino cutting (which is both exciting and inexpensive) and examples of other popular techniques such as embossing rubber stamps and using stencils.

Autumn Scene
~

You can produce interesting and complex pictures to emboss by combining several different rubber stamps. These instructions can easily be adapted to design another card using a different combination of stamps.

METHOD

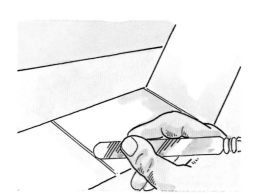

1 Score and fold the card into three sections, like a concertina – these will become the foreground, middle and background. Open the card out.

2 Using brush markers, colour directly on to the rubber surface of the posh picket stamp. Use bottle green for the fence shadow, pine green for the remainder. For the leaves, use brown, orange and ochre, blending the colours on each leaf. When fully coloured, breathe on the rubber surface of the stamp to re-moisten the ink, then stamp on to the white card all along the bottom edge of the left-hand section.

3 Colour the fence using grey and dark grey markers. Cut out all of the white area above the fence in this section only.

4 Turn the whole card over so that the fence is face down. Stamp the neighbourhood stamp centrally across the middle section. Ink the hilltop grass stamp with leaf green brush marker and stamp randomly below the houses. Now use the green marker and overstamp more grass. Use the stamp several times without re-inking to achieve shadings. Repeat using the ochre and bottle green markers.

5 Ink a sponge wedge with orange brush marker and sponge over the houses. Repeat with yellow. Using a fine black pen, draw frames at the house windows. Cut out above the houses in this section only.

6 Turn the card over so the fence is showing. On the right-hand section, stamp two tree frames using the brown and dark brown brush markers. Between these, stamp the sunshine stamp coloured with cherry, orange and yellow brush markers.

7 Ink the spring sprig stamp with leaf green and stamp randomly as for the grass, over the tree frame. Repeat with orange, ochre and brown to fill the trees.

8 Ink the sponge with cherry and sponge around the sun. Re-ink with orange and sponge around the cherry ink, repeat with orange and yellow to create a sunset.

9 Fill the remaining area, under the trees, with more grass. Re-fold the card.

Sunflower Basket

~

Using one of the many embossing kits available from craft shops, and a heat source, such as a toaster, you can easily emboss on to these rubber stamp images.

METHOD

1 Press the swirls stamp several times on to the inkstone embossing ink pad. Firmly press the stamp on to the front edge of one of the folded cards. Lift straight up and only a slight, glistening image is visible.

2 Before the embossing ink dries, sprinkle with verdigris powder. Shake off the excess. Heat the embossing powder over a toaster or using a heat gun, until it melts and rises. Repeat for all four edges.

3 Stamp and emboss the wire basket on to one side of the second card in the same way. Cut this out (including inside the handle) to leave a narrow white border.

4 Cut a rectangle 11.5 × 6cm (4½ × 2⅛in) from one side of the second card. Draw the glue pen around the edge and sprinkle with embossing powder. Heat then glue to the centre front of the swirls card.

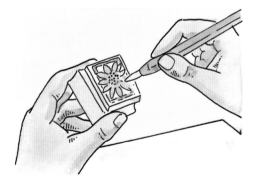

5 Using brush markers, colour the surface of the sunflower stamp – the centre brown, then edge one side of the petals only with ochre and blend with yellow. Breathe on the stamp to re-moisten, then stamp on to the back of the second piece of card. Repeat for another sunflower.

6 Cut between each petal to the centre of the flower. Place the flower face down in your hand and, using a wooden spoon handle, rub the flower on the back to curl the petals. Turn over and bend each petal up slightly. Repeat for the other flower.

7 Apply small dots of brown liquid appliqué directly from the tube to the centre section of each flower. Leave this to dry for a few hours. Heat, as if embossing, until the liquid appliqué puffs up.

8 Mount the wire basket and flowers on to the swirls card using foam tape to give a 3-D effect. For a finishing touch, tie on a gold ribbon in a bow.

MATERIALS

Sunflower Basket

~

2 pieces 23 × 15cm (9 × 6in) of white glossy card, one scored to fold in middle

•

Rubber Stampede stamps – sunflower mosaic, French wire basket and swirls

•

inkstone and verdigris embossing powders

•

brown liquid appliqué

•

brush markers – brown, ochre and yellow

•

12cm (4¾in) gold ribbon

•

craft knife

•

cutting mat

•

foam mounting tape

•

wooden spoon

•

toaster or heat gun

•

glue pen

Ducks on the Pond
~

Potato prints are fun to make, whatever your age. This card uses a combination of potato prints, paper collage, and glitter. If small children make this card, they will need help and supervision with cutting.

Ducks on the Pond
~

pale green card mount,
31 × 21.5cm (12¼ × 8½in), scored
to fold in middle
•
thick blue paper, at least as large
as the card front
•
lighter blue paper, 15 × 10cm
(6 × 4in)
•
green paper, 15 × 10cm (6 × 4in)
•
poster, gouache or acrylic paints
for the stars, flowers and ducks
•
glass or perspex surface on which
to spread paint
•
felt tip pen
•
pencil
•
ink roller
•
2 potatoes
•
scissors
•
ruler
•
craft knife or
vegetable knife
•
cutting mat
•
glitter glue, or loose glitter
and brush
•
fabric/paper glue

METHOD

1 Cut the potatoes in half. Press potatoes on to kitchen paper to dry. With a soft felt tip pen or the point of the knife, draw a star, a flower, a duck and a small square on the potato surfaces. Cut away the potato around the shapes, leaving a raised pattern.

2 Lay the folded card mount on the blue paper and draw round the edge. Then, using a ruler and pencil, draw a frame 1cm (⅜in) in from the edge of the paper. Carefully cut the frame out with the craft knife. Save the blue paper from the middle of the frame.

3 Cut wavy shapes from the lighter blue paper for the waves and sky. Cut a strip of grass and flower stems and leaves from the green paper. Glue to the mount.

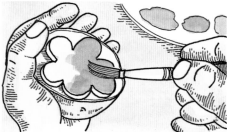

4 Paint directly on to the potato shapes or spread out the paint with roller on to glass or perspex, and dip the potato shapes into it. Press firmly on to the card mount to make a pattern. When the prints are dry, use the square cut to print the hearts of the flowers and the eyes of the ducks. Leave to dry.

5 Glue the blue paper frame to the edge of the card mount. Decorate the card with glitter glue, or spread or brush glue on the parts you would like to be glittery, and sprinkle the glitter on so that it adheres.

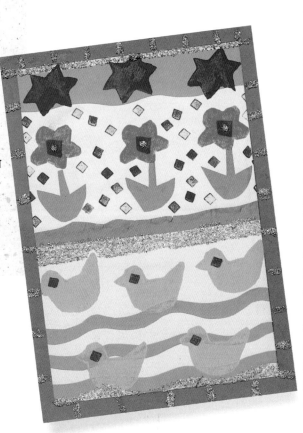

Fish and Starfish

~

Potato printing is one of the simplest of all printing techniques, usually reserved just for young children. However, with a little extra care in planning the design and choosing colours, the results can be surprisingly effective.

METHOD

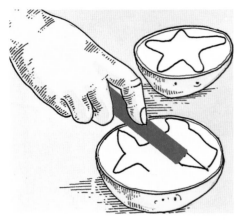

1 Cut the potato in half. Press potato halves on to kitchen paper to dry. Draw a fish on one half and a starfish on the other with a soft felt-tip or the point of the knife. Carefully cut away the parts of the design which you do not wish to print.

3 Trim the print to the size you want, and glue it on to the blue mount.

4 Print starfish around the border, using alternating colours.

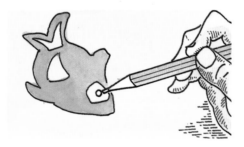

5 With the silver pen, draw a line around the edge of the fish print, and add silver dots for the fishes' eyes to make them shine.

2 Spread out the paint with roller on to a smooth surface such as glass or perspex, and dip the raised fish shape into it so that it is covered with paint. Then press the fish on to the light-coloured paper to make a print. Print other fish all over in a random pattern as if they are swimming, using different colours and cleaning the potato between each application of colour. You can use two colours of paint next to each other on the glass for multicolour fish.

Variation

Print a few fish or starfish on the envelope in which you are sending the card.

MATERIALS

Fish and Starfish
~

blue card mount, 31 × 21.5cm (12¼ × 8½in), scored to fold in middle

•

smaller yellow paper for the fish print

•

poster, gouache or acrylic paints in different colours

•

soft felt-tip pen

•

silver felt-tip pen

•

glass or perspex surface on which to spread paint

•

ink roller

•

potato

•

kitchen paper

•

craft knife or vegetable knife

Lino Print Repeat
~

For this design, the artist has used a small lino cut and printed this over and over again to build up a repeat pattern. You could also add a detail with another cut, printed in a contrasting colour.

MATERIALS

Lino Print Repeat
~

white card mount, 30 × 17cm
(12 × 6¾in), scored to fold
in middle
•
coloured card or paper cut slightly
smaller than front of mount
•
square of white paper for printing,
cut just larger than lino
•
pencils
•
tracing paper
•
small square of lino (or soft wood
if no lino is available)
•
lino-printing ink
•
sheet of glass or PVC for inking
•
ink roller
•
lino-cutting tool
•
craft knife
•
cutting mat
•
masking tape
•
glitter glue (optional)
•
fabric/paper glue

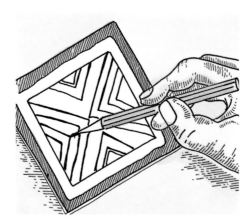

1 Draw the design for the lino cut on tracing paper. Scribble over the back of the drawing with pencil. Turn the drawing the right way over, place it on the lino and draw over the lines of the design again with a sharp pencil. This will transfer your design accurately to the lino.

METHOD

2 Tape the edges of the lino to the work surface with masking tape. Cut around your design into the lino with a lino-cutting tool. Don't forget that it is the parts which you *don't* cut that will be printed. Hold the lino-cutting tool with two hands and rest your arms on the work surface, so that you have more control of the tool. Always cut away from you and *take care*, as the lino-cutting tool will be very sharp. (It's a good idea to practise on a spare piece of lino first.)

3 Squeeze some ink on to the piece of glass or similar surface. Roll the roller in the ink so that it is evenly covered. Then roll the ink evenly over the lino cut.

4 Hold the square of lino carefully by the edges and press it down on to the square of white paper as if you were using a stamp. Repeat this process, inking the lino each time, and carefully lining up the prints. Here, the cut has been given a quarter-turn each time, so that the pattern alternates.

5 When the finished print is dry, mount it on to the coloured paper and decorate this with dots of glitter glue, if desired. Glue the paper on to the card mount.

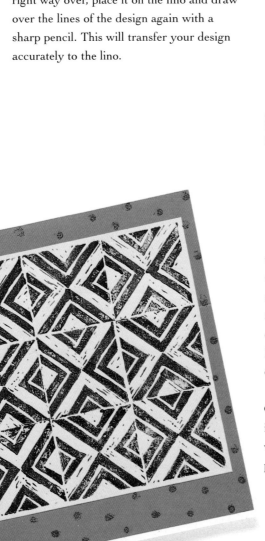

Christmas Lino Print
~

For this design a single lino cut has been made for the whole picture. The card is printed in a slightly different way from the Lino Print Repeat, which used a stamping method, and has been hand-tinted using coloured inks.

METHOD

1 Follow Steps 1–3 from the previous card. You can trace a collage of images from books and magazines, or draw your own.

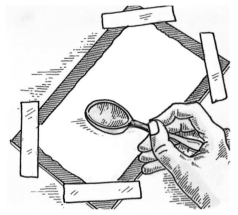

2 With the inked lino still fixed to the work surface with masking tape, lay the tissue, or other paper, over the lino, and very carefully press down, taking care not to move the paper. Tape the paper to the lino or work surface at the corners, and gently rub over the back of the paper with the back of a spoon. This will make the images in the picture clearer.

3 Remove the paper from the lino, making sure you do not smudge the print, and allow to dry.

4 Tint some areas of the print with the inks, allowing the colours to run into each other, and allowing some colours to be more intense than others.

5 Mount the tissue print on to the white paper and then carefully tear the paper around the print, leaving a narrow border of white. The soft, irregular edge of the tissue gives the image a sense of movement and the uneven border around the edge of the lino print adds a touch of interest.

6 Mount the finished design on to the coloured card mount using PVA glue.

MATERIALS

Christmas Lino Print
~

coloured card mount, 30 × 21cm (12 × 8½in), scored to fold in middle

•

soft white paper to mount picture

•

white tissue, or a soft paper which gives an interesting ripped edge, for printing image

•

tracing paper

•

piece of lino cut to size of required image

•

metal spoon

•

lino-printing ink

•

coloured inks

•

sheet of glass or PVC for inking

•

ink roller

•

paintbrush

•

lino-cutting tool

•

masking tape

•

PVA glue

Silkscreen Print
~

This richly coloured card is produced with stencils and a silkscreen. As the colours are printed separately, you must make a stencil for each colour. It is important that these stencils are accurately traced from the master drawing if the colours are to be correctly positioned. When tracing, use a lightbox or a window pane. Registration – positioning the different parts of the design so they don't overlap – can be difficult, so make sure your design is fairly open with spaces to see through.

METHOD

1 Make a clear, accurate drawing and colour-code it, using the template on p125.

2 Trace a stencil for each colour from newsprint and cut, using the craft knife. Save the cut-out pieces. These can be put back into place when printing other colours. Where necessary, leave small spaces between the cutting areas, which will help to keep the stencil whole. Make sure that the stencil is large enough to fill the screen, or the colour will come through along the gap at the sides.

3 Clean and tape the edges of the screen to required size with gummed tape. Prepare dry silk for printing by stretching it on cardboard with masking tape – taut fabric gives the best results.

4 Mix printing dyes according to manufacturer's instructions.

5 When ready, position stencil over the silk, ready to print with the first colour. Any areas that you *don't* want to print should be masked by replacing the cut-out pieces in the stencil. Lay the screen on top.

6 Using a spoon, pour the colour along the top edge of the screen and use the squeegie to pull the colour firmly down across the screen twice. You may need help to hold the screen down.

7 Remove the screen carefully. Wash the equipment to make it ready for the next colour. When the colours are dry, repeat the process with subsequent stencils.

8 After printing is complete and the colours are dry, remove the fabric and iron on the back to fix the colours. Score mount to fold in middle. Cut print along the edges and fix to mount with iron-on adhesive.

Variation
By using only one of the stencils and different colours, you achieve a very different effect.

Shell Print with Ribbon Tie

~

It's possible to make a great variety of cards using this method. Look in antique book shops for old prints – images from old cookbooks work well. Alternatively, photocopy black-and-white drawings from books (make sure they're out of copyright). Cut the drawings out, mount them together, perhaps numbering or naming each item, and reduce on a photocopier to the size you want. Don't forget that you can easily photocopy on to coloured paper.

METHOD

MATERIALS

Shell Print with Ribbon Tie

~

card mount, 21 × 15cm (8¼ × 6in), scored to fold in middle

•

photocopied print, reduced and cut to size

•

small shell

•

diluted instant coffee

•

coloured pencils

•

paintbrush

•

ribbon

•

craft knife

•

cutting mat

•

fabric/paper glue

•

all-purpose adhesive

1 Brush the diluted coffee on to the print to "antique" it. Leave to dry.

3 Glue on the shell with all-purpose adhesive. Write your message, then tie a ribbon around the card to give it the feeling of a special gift.

2 Use coloured pencils to tint the print. Apply a thin layer of paper glue to the back of the print and quickly press it in place on the card mount. (It's useful to put pencil registration marks on the mount for the corners so that you can get it in the right position quickly.)

Stripy Butterflies
~

Look for photographs or illustrations of bright or unusual butterflies in magazines or old books, and cut them out to decorate this card.

METHOD

1 Paint one piece of card dark blue, and the second piece red. Sponge over.

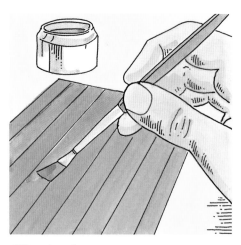

2 When dry, paint stripes in various shades of green over the red.

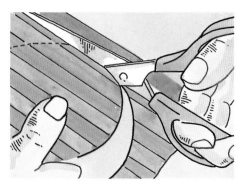

3 With a compass, draw a circle on to the red and green card. Cut out and glue on to the dark blue card.

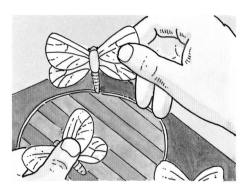

4 Arrange butterflies on the card, and glue into place.

5 Using gold felt-tip pen, draw carefully around the red and green circle.

Variation
Use different butterflies and background for another finish.

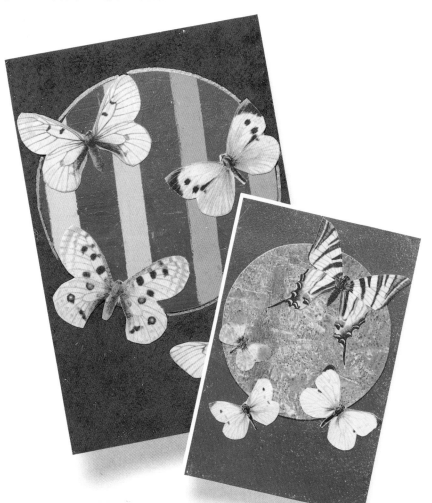

Leaf Print
~

Use a colour photocopier to create an original and personal design. You can copy fresh leaves as well as dried: red and yellow autumn leaves look particularly striking.

METHOD

1 Arrange the leaves on the paper and attach them lightly with double-sided tape, or a spot of glue. Cover the picture with acetate and tape this to the backing paper at the edges with masking tape. The acetate protects the image and need not be removed when copying.

2 Have a colour laser copy made, reducing the picture to fit. Cut this out and glue it to the front of the card mount.

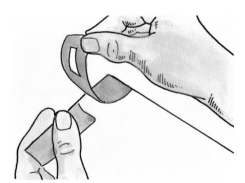

3 Tear a band along a cut edge of the contrasting paper. After signing the card, fix the paper band around it using double-sided tape at the back, so the band can slide off.

Get Fruity
~

You could experiment with the many 3-D painting craft products available, although this card was made with painter's modelling paste.

METHOD

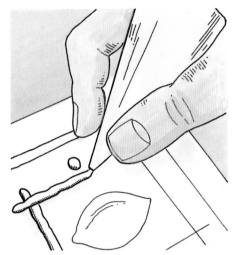

1 Put modelling paste in the piping bag, cut the corner off the bag and use the plain nozzle to pipe the 3-D pattern on to the card mount – you may like to draw your picture with pencil first.

2 Allow the paste to dry for several hours, following the manufacturer's instructions, then paint the fruit with a water-based paint.

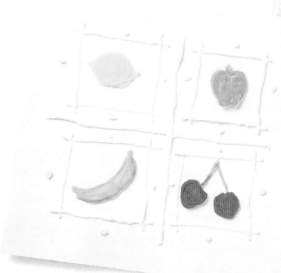

MATERIALS

Leaf Print
~
card mount, 21 × 15cm
[8¼ × 6in], scored to fold in middle

•

paper for mounting, same size as front of mount

•

sheet of acetate

•

contrasting paper for band

•

selection of fresh or pressed leaves

•

double-sided and masking tapes

•

craft knife

•

cutting mat

•

paper glue

Get Fruity
~
card mount, 31 × 14.5cm
[12¼ × 5¾in], scored to fold in middle

•

painters' acrylic modelling paste

•

strong piping bag for cake decorating, with plain nozzle

•

water-based paints – watercolour, acrylic gouache etc.

•

craft knife

•

cutting mat

Gallery

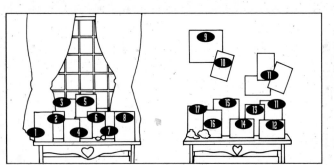

1 Teatime
Judy Caplin
This paper is given a wash with inks and watercolours and the teapot is drawn in with fine pen and ink.

2 Christmas Glitter
Personal Stamp Exchange
A very detailed combination of embossed rubber stamp images, carefully coloured and bordered with more stamps.

3 Marbled Card
Charlotte Lapstich
This hand-marbled card is made using traditional techniques dating back 1000 years.

4 Pear/Christmas Stocking
Chowwai Cheung
These delicate hand-painted images are mounted on embossed handmade paper backgrounds.

5 Sunflower Seeds
Wendy Mackenzie
Hand-coloured rubber stamps of a flower and a bee are printed on to the card mount and an attached seed packet.

6 Sitting on Top of the World
Sousan Luqman
Hand-coloured rubber stamps of the globe on its stand form a background for the hand-drawn, cut-out angel and banner.

7 Double Sun

Underground Art
The designer of this card uses an original and unique process involving ceramic materials to create 3D embossed images.

8 Native American Bird

Personal Stamp Exchange
This rubber stamp image of a bird is embossed and cut out, then hung by thread against an interesting mixture of paper backgrounds.

9 Vegetable Garden

Personal Stamp Exchange
Hand-coloured and embossed vegetable stamps are printed on to paper finished with decorative-edged scissors.

10 Easter Eggs

Kate Twelvetrees
This card uses cut-out colour photocopies, mounted on coloured paper, covered with tissue paper and tied with raffia.

11 Peacock/Three Wise Men/Seahorses/Primitive Men

Julie Hammond
Hand-printed lino cuts are used in a variety of images, both simple and complex.

12 Flower and Print

Thérèse McDermott
This appliquéd fabric card has a handwritten and printed acetate background.

13 Chocolate Cake

Wendy Mackenzie
The cake on this card is printed using chocolate.

14 My Love is like a Red, Red Rose

Kate Twelvetrees
Antiqued photocopies and a dried rose make a lovely Valentine.

15 Dolphin Bay

Michael Bossom
Rubber-stamped dolphins border the central image which is created with encaustic art – a technique that paints with hot coloured wax.

16 Sparkler

Kate Twelvetrees
The black and white photocopy is from a nineteenth-century print. The card also used a burnt-out sparkler firework, painted gold and wrapped with gold thread.

17 Heart and Words

Hand and Heart Design
Chinese gold and silver-covered tissue papers form frames for the heart and the print mounted on handmade paper backgrounds.

Stripy Flowers
~

two pieces of card, 20 × 15cm
(8 × 6in)
•
cut-out flower motifs
•
acrylic paint in cream and two
tones of blue (or two tones of
another colour)
•
gold felt-tip pen
•
small paintbrush
•
craft knife
•
cutting mat
•
paper glue

Wrapped Colour Print
~

card mount, 21 × 15cm (8¼ × 6in),
scored to fold in middle
•
colour laser print
•
fine white tissue paper
•
contrasting paper for the band
•
craft knife
•
cutting mat
•
double-sided tape
•
paper glue

Stripy Flowers
~

*Magazines or gardening catalogues will provide
a rich source of pictures for the central motifs
of these cards.*

METHOD

1 Paint two pieces of card in the two
tones of blue.

2 Paint cream stripes on the lighter blue
card. Leave to dry.

3 Arrange the flower motifs on the
striped card, and glue into place.

4 Carefully paint cream dots between
lines with the small paintbrush.

5 Fold the darker blue card in two.
Using the craft knife and cutting mat, cut
out a frame from this front half. Glue the
decorated card in place behind it.

6 Using the gold felt-tip pen, draw two
lines framing the flower motifs. Draw gold
dots in the middle of the cream dots.

Wrapped Colour Print
~

*Wrapping a colour laser copy in tissue can
make the drawing beneath look like an original.
This pear is a detail from a nineteenth-century
hand-coloured engraving. Seal the card with a
toning paper band after you have signed it, to
complete your gift.*

METHOD

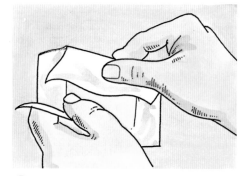

1 Cut the colour laser copy to size and
wrap it in tissue, gluing the tissue to the
back of the print. Glue the tissue parcel to
the mount.

2 Tear a band from the edge of the
contrasting paper, leaving one cut edge.
After you have signed the card, secure
the band round the card using double-
sided tape at the back so that the band
can slide off.

Two-tone Ferns

~

Use feathery fern shapes to make this simple card in two contrasting colours.

METHOD

Variation

1 Draw a pencil line down the middle of one of the cards. Paint one half black and the other cream. Sponge over for interesting texture.

2 Arrange ferns in the centre of the card. Use rolled-up masking tape to keep the ferns in place or hold them firmly with your hand.

3 Sponge black paint over the fern on the cream side of the card, and cream paint over the fern on the black side. When dry, remove the ferns.

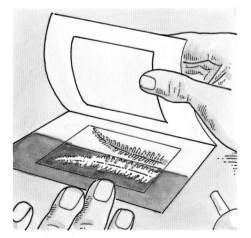

4 Fold the second piece of card and, using the craft knife and cutting mat, cut out a frame from the front half. Paint one half black and the other half cream. Place over the fern design, and glue into place.

Baby Clothes

~

Flocking powders are available from craft shops. The powder is usually sprinkled over a glued surface, but double-sided adhesive film has been used here.

METHOD

1 Cut a piece of film the same size as the front of the mount. Peel off backing and stick to the mount. Draw the outlines of baby clothes directly on to the film.

2 Cut round the shapes you have drawn with a craft knife, taking care to cut only through the release paper. Peel off the background of the picture leaving the objects covered. Sprinkle the card with the darkest flocking powder, gently rubbing it on to the film with your finger. Shake off excess.

3 Colour code the objects and peel the release paper off one colour at a time, sprinkling each shape in the same way. Overlapping light colours on to the dark background gives a halo effect which softens the image.

MATERIALS

Two-tone Ferns

~

two pieces of card, 20 × 15cm
[8 × 6in]

•

ferns

•

acrylic paint in black and cream
[or two other contrasting colours]

•

paintbrush

•

small synthetic sponge

•

craft knife

•

cutting mat

•

masking tape

•

paper glue

•

pencil

Baby Clothes

~

card mount, 21 × 15cm
[8¹/₄ × 6in], scored to fold at top

•

double-sided self-adhesive film

•

3 light coloured and one dark
coloured flocking powders

•

craft knife

•

cutting mat

Stencilled Hearts
~

You can buy stencils in many different shapes – but it's very easy to make your own.
A homemade stencil can be cut to any design you choose.

Stencilled Hearts
~

white card mount, 30 × 18cm
[12 × 7in], scored to fold
in middle
•
piece of card slightly smaller than
front of card mount
•
2 different-coloured papers smaller
than piece of card, one slightly
larger than the other
•
large piece stiff stencil card
•
kitchen foil to cover card
•
acrylic paints
•
sponge
•
old toothbrush
•
craft knife
•
cutting mat
•
paper glue
•
PVA glue

METHOD

1 Cut a heart-shaped window in the stiff card to make a stencil (see page 124).

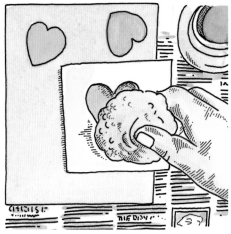

2 Place the stencil on the smaller of the pieces of coloured paper. Press the sponge into the paint and test for density of colour on a piece of scrap paper. Then, holding the stencil down firmly, press the sponge over the stencil. Allow to dry.

3 Place the stencil in a different position and spatter over it. To do this, dab the old toothbrush into fairly dry paint, and flick the brush over the stencil. Build up a pattern of hearts over the mount, some sponged and some spattered.

4 Spatter a little pale-coloured paint over the hearts and the background. Trim the composition if necessary.

5 Spatter the slightly larger piece of coloured paper in a contrasting colour.

6 Cover the piece of card with the foil, folding it over the edges of the card, and gluing it in place behind with PVA.

7 Using paper glue, fix the foil-covered card to the mount, then the spattered paper, and finally the heart print.

Wax Crayon Heart
~

This simple but effective technique is fun for all ages, and is a good method if you want fine detail.
The heart-shaped window mount of this card frames the image in an unusual way.

METHOD

1 Cover the whole surface of the paper with different coloured wax crayons in any random pattern you like.

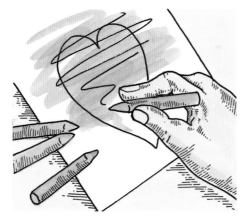

2 Now cover the coloured surface with black wax crayon.

3 Using the tip of the used ballpoint pen, draw a heart shape into the black wax crayon and scrape out a pattern revealing the colours beneath.

4 Trace the shape of the patterned heart, and transfer this outline to the front of the card mount. Cut out the heart-shaped window with scissors. Rub out any pencil marks.

5 Spread glue along the inside edges of the window and press down in place around the coloured heart. Make sure that the edge of the window is properly glued down all the way along. Glue the piece of blue lining card to the back of the coloured heart to cover it.

6 Decorate the front of the card with a simple pattern in black ink, if you wish.

Variation
Try making similar cards using different images, such as a simple star or flower. If you made the images smaller, you could even use two or more on the same card, either repeating a single design or combining different ones.

MATERIALS

Wax Crayon Heart
~

blue card mount, 21 × 12.5cm [8¼ × 5in], scored to fold in middle

•

white card or paper, same size as front of card mount

•

blue card to line inside front of card mount

•

tracing paper

•

wax crayons in bright colours, and black

•

used ballpoint pen

•

eraser

•

scissors

•

craft knife

•

cutting mat

•

fabric/paper glue

MATERIALS

3-D Pearly Heart
~

orange card mount, 28 × 14cm
(11 × 5½in), scored to fold in
middle

•

white card, 4.5 sq cm (1¾ sq in)

•

3-D pearl fabric paint in
different colours

•

scissors or craft knife

•

cutting mat

•

fabric/paper glue

Stencilled Sun Face
~

cream-coloured card, 18 × 18cm
(7 × 7in)

•

thick stencil card, 20 × 20cm
(8 × 8in)

•

tracing paper

•

old newspaper

•

gold and bronze spray paints

•

craft knife

•

cutting mat

•

metal ruler

•

magic tape

•

template
(page 125)

3-D Pearly Heart
~

*Using 3-D pearlized fabric paint, you can
squeeze out a glossy, raised pattern on to card,
with a pleasing irregularity of line.*

METHOD

1 Squeeze out a pearlized fabric paint
heart shape in the centre of the white card.
Working outwards from the heart, build up
your own pattern using different colours
leaving a white border around your design.
Leave to dry long enough for the card to be
handled.

2 Glue the square to the orange card
mount, placing it in the centre.

3 Squeeze out a border in green along
the white edges of the white square. Then,
working outwards, build up a wide,
patterned border in other colours on the
orange card. Allow the card to dry for 24
hours.

Stencilled Sun Face
~

*This beautifully designed stencil makes a very
impressive card. The spray paint gives a
textured look, of the quality of old gold.
Accurate cutting of the sun's rays is essential,
so use a sharp knife – but be careful.*

METHOD

1 Trace the sun design from the template
on to stencil card. Using the ruler, craft
knife and a cutting mat, cut away all the
areas that are shaded on the template.

2 Cover the surrounding area with
newspaper. Place the stencil over the card
and tape in place with magic tape. Spray
lightly with gold paint, then with bronze to
fall mainly on the right-hand side of the
stencil.

3 When the paint has dried, remove the
stencil and cut out the rays of the sun with
a craft knife.

Safety Warning
*Always use spray paints according to the manufacturer's
instructions in a well-ventilated room and avoid inhaling
them.*

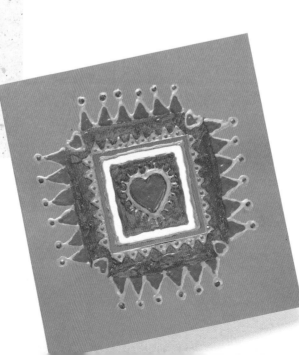

Flying Hearts
~

Printing with rubber stamps is another method of relief printing, like potato cuts. There are thousands of wonderful rubber stamps available, but you can make your own stamp by following this easy method. Simple shapes printed again and again to create a repeat pattern can look very effective. It works well on a small scale – the front of this card measures 9 × 12cm (3½ × 4½in).

METHOD

1 In felt pen, draw a simple shape, such as a small heart with wings, on the rubber. To prevent the rubber moving while you cut it, attach it to the mat using masking tape on all four sides. *Do not* hold the rubber while cutting. Using the craft knife, cut away the rubber around the shape to a depth of about 3mm (⅛in).

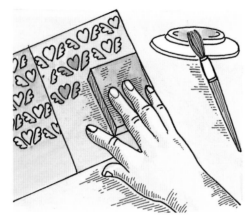

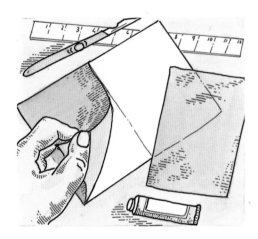

2 Cut two pieces of tissue paper to fit the front and back of the card mount. The front should be a different colour from the back. Carefully glue the tissue in place using PVA, smoothing out any wrinkles.

3 Use purchased ink pads, already impregnated with gold and silver inks; or apply water-based gold and silver inks to a flat kitchen sponge. Press the rubber stamp into the gold pad or paint gold on to the stamp, test on a piece of paper, then stamp a pattern all over the front and back of the card mount.

4 Clean the rubber stamp and cover the stamp with silver paint, then overprint silver on the shape in the centre front of the card.

back

front

Variation
You could stamp a single print inside the card, and one on the flap of the envelope, to look like a seal.

Batik Print
~

This is an unusual way of using a well-known technique. Dye a larger piece of cloth and then cut out your favourite sections of the design to frame as cards, using card in a toning colour.

METHOD

1 Secure cloth on a flat surface with masking tape. Lay newspaper on the surface to protect it from hot wax.

2 Heat the wax in a saucepan according to the manufacturer's instructions. Draw on to the cloth with the melted wax using a tjanting – the waxed areas will remain white. Allow to dry.

3 Mix the pink dye in a bowl and leave the cloth to soak for the time given in instructions. Remove and rinse in cold water. Allow to dry.

4 Tape dry fabric as in Step 1. Apply wax to the areas to remain pink either with the tjanting or by dripping. Allow to dry.

5 Place cloth in a bowl with blue dye and leave as before. Rinse and leave to dry.

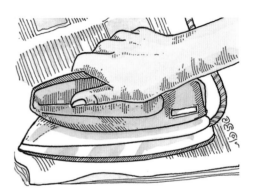

6 To remove the wax, first pick off as much as possible, then place newspaper under and over dyed cloth and iron carefully. The heat should melt the remaining wax, which will then be absorbed by the paper.

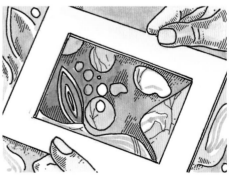

7 Cut out the desired piece of design and cut a window mount in the white card to fit. Cut a second window mount in the front of the card mount, making the window slightly larger so that a border of white is left around the print. Glue the mounts and the print together.

Classic Vase

~

The colours and bold patterns of this design are reminiscent of the ancient world. Look in your library for books showing old ornamental details – Egyptian, Greek or Celtic designs perhaps – which could be simplified to make stencils, lino cuts, etc.

MATERIALS

Classic Vase
~

black card mount, 32 × 19cm (12½ × 7½in), scored to fold in middle

•

black card for window mount, same size as front of mount

•

stencil card

•

tracing paper

•

calico, slightly smaller than front of mount, and spare strips

•

gold and black fabric pens, or gold and black paint and paintbrushes

•

pinking scissors, or other scissors with a decorative edge

•

craft knife

•

cutting mat

•

masking tape

•

fabric/paper glue

•

template

METHOD

1 Trace design from the template on page 122 on to the stencil card. Ordinary card can be used, but oiled stencil card can be used again and again.

2 Cut the shapes out carefully with the craft knife, on the cutting mat.

3 Attach the stencil with masking tape to the calico. With the fabric pen, or brush and paint, fill in the black areas. Hold the stencil down to stop the paint seeping underneath.

4 Allow to dry and fill in the gold areas in the same way.

5 Cut a window mount from the black card to fit around your stencilled design. Apply glue to the back of the mount and press it down in place on the calico.

6 Paint some spare calico gold and cut into strips for the border. Trim one long edge of each strip with the pinking scissors.

7 Glue the gold calico strips to the black frame. Glue the print and frame to the front of your card mount.

Introduction

All you need is a sharp pair of scissors and a craft knife! There are many kinds of papercraft and the techniques described here range from very simple torn shapes to cunning 3-D cards. If you enjoy making the pop-up and moving cards in this section, explore ephemera markets for different versions of pop-up cards that you can examine and copy. Remember childhood activities — rows of paper cut-out dolls, cutting "doilies", making paper chains at Christmas — adapt all the ideas you can. You can also experiment with tearing paper — textured or handmade papers reveal soft, feathery edges against darker backgrounds. Another increasingly popular technique is paper casting, demonstrated on

page 80. Visit specialist artists' and printers' paper shops and look particularly **Papercraft**

at handmade papers containing natural materials such as flowers or straw.

If paper cutting and collages really excite you, make your own paper using the simple methods described in paper-making books — each sheet made

will create more than one card and be truly individual. And you can experiment with the vivid colours of fabric dyes and printing inks.

Heart through the Window
~

You could use this technique to frame any interesting small image. For this particular card, tissue paper has been used for the heart so that it glows like stained glass when seen against the light. The blue also provides a vivid contrast to the orange.

MATERIALS

Heart through the Window
~

2 strips of coloured paper in slightly different colours, each measuring approximately 72 × 16cm (28 × 6¼in)

•

small piece of blue paper approximately 2.5 × 3cm (1 × 1¼in)

•

piece of blue tissue, slightly smaller than blue paper rectangle

•

iron-on adhesive or low-tack self-adhesive sheet

•

scissors

•

craft knife

•

cutting board

•

PVA glue

METHOD

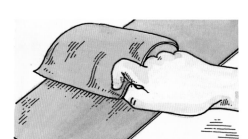

1 Using an iron-on adhesive or a low-tack adhesive sheet and following the manufacturer's instructions, fix the two long pieces of paper together.

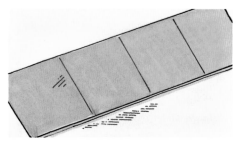

2 Score the strip lightly in three places so that you can fold and concertina the strip into four equal sides, each 18cm (7in) wide.

3 Now cut irregularly shaped rectangular windows from the mount by marking the corners and then draw in the sides of the first and largest window on the front of the mount with a pencil. Cut out this shape, approximately 8 × 9cm (3¼ × 3½in) wide, with scissors. Cut three more windows in the same way on each layer of the mount: they should become increasingly smaller so that the window in the back of the mount measures approximately 2 × 2.5cm (¾ × 1in).

4 Use the off-cuts of paper to make contrasting borders around the front and third windows.

5 Cut a tiny window in the shape of a heart from the blue paper and glue the blue tissue behind this. Apply a little glue to the edges of the smallest window on the back of the mount and press on to the blue paper.

Bon Voyage
~

Use this simple method to create pop-up cards for all kinds of events.

METHOD

1 Fold the white card in half. Draw plane and message banner lightly in pencil on the inside, with the fold line running vertically through the centre of both.

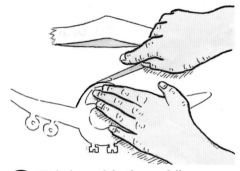

2 With the craft knife, carefully cut around the body of the plane, taking care not to cut through the sides of the body that meet the wings. In the same way, cut along the top and bottom edges of the banner, leaving the two ends uncut.

4 Gently pull the cut-out shapes forward so that they fold in the opposite direction from the centre fold. Fold the card.

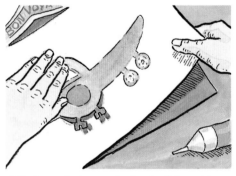

5 Spread glue on the back of the white card, leaving the cut-out sections unglued. Press in place on the blue card.

3 Paint the plane and the banner, rubbing out any pencil marks. Allow to dry.

Stand-up Goose
~

Explore your local library for nineteenth-century folk-art illustrations and woodcuts which you could adapt to make other stand-up cards.

MATERIALS

Stand-up Goose
~

white card, 23 × 15cm (9 × 6in)
•
tracing paper
•
artist's masking fluid
•
gouache or watercolour paints
•
fine paintbrush
•
small natural sponge
•
craft knife
•
cutting mat
•
fabric/paper glue
•
acrylic gloss or matt varnish and diffuser (optional)

METHOD

1 Trace the outline from the template (see p122) on to the card, allowing room to cut out the triangle in Step 4. Paint the areas that you want to remain white with masking fluid, and allow to dry.

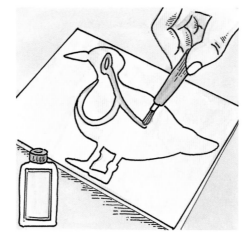

2 Use a small sponge to apply the paint, carefully filling in each area, and allowing each colour to dry before applying the next. Don't worry too much about going outside the main outline, as this will be trimmed. Paint in the eye with a fine brush. When the paint is dry, rub off the masking fluid.

3 Cut out the goose shape with a craft knife on a cutting mat.

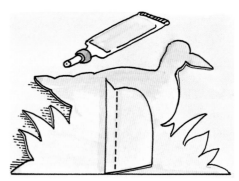

4 Cut a 10cm (4in) stand for the card, angling the short edge as shown. Score 1cm (½in) in from the long edge. Fold back along the score line, and glue on to the back of the goose.

5 For a shiny finish, or simply to protect the surface, varnish the painted goose using a diffuser and acrylic gloss or matt varnish.

Variation
You can also make a stand-up card from a photograph of a favourite object or toy. Photograph it against a white or plain background, enlarge the photo, and carefully cut out around the object.

Stand-up Pig
~

You could make your own template by tracing pictures or photographs of other animals from books or magazines. If you want a larger template, enlarge the image on a photocopier.

METHOD

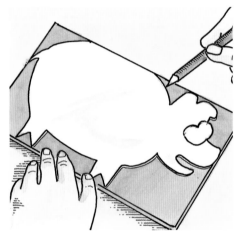

❶ Fold the pink card in half lengthways, and lay the template (see page 123) on the card so that the back of the pig is on the fold. Draw around the template, and cut out the pig shape.

❷ Glue on two white circles of card for the eyes.

❸ Draw on details either in pencils or with felt-tip pens.

3-D Star
~

This card has been made with thin card with tissue paper glued to both sides to create an interesting mottled effect. Another way to achieve a similar result is to buy thin card with a texture or pattern.

METHOD

❶ Following the manufacturer's instructions, use the double-sided film or iron-on adhesive to cover both sides of the cards with dark blue tissue.

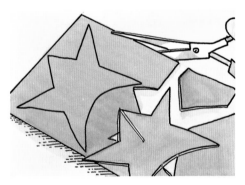

❷ Using the template (see page 123), cut out two stars from the tissue-covered card. Make a slit in one star from the bottom to the centre and in the other from the top to the centre, as shown on the template. Slot the two stars together.

❸ Lay the star flat on the work surface. Use the iron-on adhesive to cover just the side facing you (it doesn't matter which side) with the light-coloured tissue. The tissue will cover the slits where the two stars join, preventing the two stars from slipping apart, and providing a lighter-coloured side on which to write a message.

❹ Glue the small silver stars on to the sides covered in dark blue tissue.

MATERIALS

Stand-up Pig
~

pink card, 25 × 18cm (7 × 10in)
•
tracing paper
•
scrap of white card
•
coloured pencils or felt tips
•
craft knife
•
cutting mat
•
paper glue

3-D Star
~

two squares of thin card, 20 × 20cm (8 × 8in)
•
dark blue tissue to cover
•
light blue tissue for "inside" of card
•
packet of small silver stars
•
double-sided self-adhesive film or iron-on adhesive
•
scissors

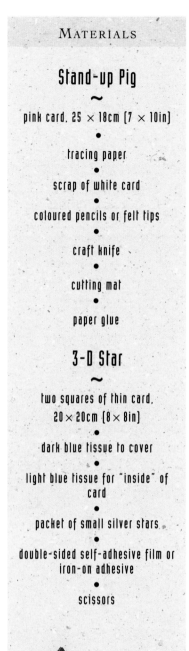

Pop-up Sun, Bee and Flowers
~

This cheerful card makes an intriguing summer birthday gift.

MATERIALS

Pop-up Sun, Bee and Flowers
~

2 pieces strong green card,
15 × 15cm (6 × 6in)

•

2 pieces strong blue card
15 × 15cm (6 × 6in)

•

yellow and white paper

•

thick, strong blue cotton thread

•

craft knife

•

cutting mat

•

sellotape

•

fabric/paper glue

•

all-purpose adhesive

METHOD

back

1 Put the edge of one blue card abutting the edge of a green card and stick them together with tape. Repeat with another two cards, then fold them together with the tape on the inside. Keep the cards open. Cut out each of the green cards, one in the shape of grass with a shrub on the right, one with a tree on the left. Make sure the fold is on the base and the grass about 6cm (2½in) high with Card Two having grass over only two-thirds of the front (see above).

2 On the back of a blue card, make two horizontal parallel cuts, from the middle of the card to the grass side – one cut 1cm (⅜in), the other 2cm (¾in) from the base.

3 On the back of Card Two, make two vertical parallel 1.5cm (⅝in) cuts starting .5cm (³⁄₁₆in) from the base, 3cm (1⅛in) and 4cm (1½in) from the outside edge. Slot the grass side of the first card inside that of the second.

4 Open the cards out and thread the long, thin strip of Card One through the first slit of Card Two and back in through the second slit. Tape the loose end of the cut-out strip closed, covering about 1cm (⅜in) of the card. Pull the cards apart as far as they will go.

5 Make three little flowers by cutting out a clover shape from white paper with a small circle of yellow for the centres. Draw and cut out a sun and a bee. With the card still folded out, face down and flat, place the flowers and bee face down between the two shrubs.

6 Stick a piece of blue cotton thread with a strong all-purpose adhesive from the middle of one shrub to the flowers and the bee and then to the second shrub. Make sure the thread is as tight as possible and leave to dry. Repeat with the sun but at a higher position.

7 When dry, put some more glue on the tip of each shrub and fold the back and front together. Let the card dry then push the two halves together – the flowers, bee and sun will fall down behind the grass unseen.

Sun through Clouds
~

Pull apart these two grey clouds . . . and the sun will come shining through.

METHOD

1 Fold the two pieces of card in half lengthways. Draw and paint cloud shapes on the front of each piece, with the fold forming the base of each cloud. Cut out.

2 On the back of one of the cloud cards, make two horizontal parallel cuts from the middle of the card to the inner edge of the cloud, where it will touch the sun. One cut should be 1cm (½in) from the fold at the base, the other cut should be 2cm (1in) from the fold.

3 On the back of the second cloud card, make two vertical parallel cuts 1.5cm (¾in) long, starting 5mm (¼in) from the fold. The first cut should be about 3cm (1¼in) in from the sun side of the cloud, the second about 4cm (1½in) in.

4 With the inner sun sides together, slide the card with the horizontal cuts into the card with the vertical cuts. Open the cards out and thread the horizontal strip of the inner out and back in through the two vertical slits on the outer card.

5 Tape the loose end of the horizontal strip back to the main body of the inner card. This will prevent the inner card sliding right out of the outer card.

6 Pull the cards apart as far as they will go, and measure the space between them about 2–3cm (¾–1¼in) from the top of the clouds. Draw a sun, with rays, on the yellow card slightly larger than this measurement. Paint or draw in the features, and cut out.

7 With the cards still opened out, and face down at full extension, place the sun, face down, between the front of the two cards, in the place it would be when risen.

8 Join the sun to the clouds: glue a length of thread from 3cm (1¼in) below the top of one cloud to the middle of the sun, to 3cm (1¼in) below the top of the second cloud. Make sure the thread is as straight as possible, with no slack. Leave to dry.

9 Dab glue near the top of each cloud inside the back and front, fold the cloud shapes back again, and press the tops together to close. Leave to dry, then slide the two clouds together.

MATERIALS

Sun through Clouds
~

**2 pieces white card, 30 × 25cm
[12 × 10in]**
•
yellow card
•
**watercolour, gouache or acrylic
paints for clouds and sun, or
coloured pencils**
•
paintbrush [if using paints]
•
strong thread
•
scissors
•
craft knife
•
cutting mat
•
sticky or masking tape
•
fabric/paper glue

New Baby Jacket
~

Stand this baby jacket up and you can rock it gently from side to side. The idea would also work well with cut-out shapes of animals. If you don't have a puncher which can make holes of varying sizes, use a paper hole puncher for the ribbon holes and cut small diamond shapes in the card with a craft knife for a decorative effect.

MATERIALS

New Baby Jacket
~

blue card, 30 × 18cm (12 × 7in)
•
yellow paper, 18 × 15cm (7 × 6in)
•
white card, 18 × 15cm (7 × 6in)
•
1m (1yd) pink satin ribbon, 5mm (¼in) wide
•
2 matching pink ready-made bows
•
4 animal-shaped buttons
•
needle and thread
•
pencil
•
hole puncher
•
scissors
•
craft knife
•
cutting mat
•
sellotape
•
paper glue

METHOD

1 Make a template in white card for the jacket. Fold the blue card in half lengthways, and lay on the template so that the fold is on the neckline of the jacket. Cut another slightly smaller jacket shape from the yellow paper.

2 On the front of the jacket, mark a punch hole pattern with the pencil, and then punch out the holes.

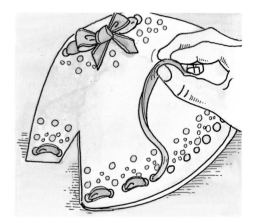

3 Thread pink satin ribbon through the large holes at the base, neck and sleeves of the jacket (wrapping a small piece of sellotape round the end of the ribbon makes this easier). Secure the ends of the ribbon at the back with a little glue. Glue the two pink satin bows at the neck and bottom of the jacket.

4 Mark where the four buttons are to be placed on the front of the jacket, and punch holes at these points. Push the button backs through the holes and, with a needle and thread, join the buttons together on the back of the jacket. Secure the buttons and thread with sellotape.

5 Carefully glue the yellow paper shape to the inside front of the jacket to neaten it.

World of Clay
~

Although the world is modelled from clay, much of the interest of this card is in the paper cutting.

METHOD

1 Mould the shape of the world out of the modelling clay then model the outlines of the continents and the lines of longitude and latitude. Leave to harden.

2 Fold the blue card into three equal sections. On the top section, draw a diagonal line from the top right hand corner to the bottom left hand corner of the top layer. Cut along the line.

3 Repeat with the other end section so that the two sections meet in a diagonal.

4 Place the world in the centre of the card and trace around it on to the two flaps. Remove the world and cut out the shape along the traced line.

5 Paint the hardened clay world and, when dry, give it a coat of clear varnish. Stick in position in the centre of the card.

Fluffy-tailed Cat
~

Many different variations of this card are possible. The cat's tail will hang over the edge of the shelf on which the card is standing – the longer the tail, the better.

METHOD

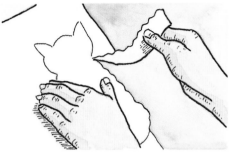

1 Lightly draw the rear outline of a cat on the watercolour paper. Tear carefully around this line – the soft paper gives the impression of fur. Erase pencil marks.

2 Glue the cat on to the front of the mount, so that its bottom touches the bottom edge of the mount. Apply a thin line of all-purpose adhesive around the neck of the cat and press the stones on to this.

3 Glue the end of the maribou trimming near the bottom of the card for the tail.

MATERIALS

World of Clay
~

blue card, 21 × 30cm [12 × 8¼in]

•

self-hardening modelling clay

•

acrylic or water-based poster paint

•

modelling tool – a cocktail stick, flat-ended knife or teaspoon handle

•

clear varnish

•

all-purpose adhesive

Fluffy-tailed Cat
~

card mount, 21 × 15cm [8¼ × 6in], scored to fold in middle

•

soft watercolour paper

•

small fake gemstones

•

30cm [12in] maribou trimming

•

pencil and eraser

•

fabric/paper glue

•

all-purpose adhesive

Gallery

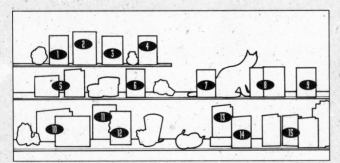

1 Fossil Fish
Helen Rowan
This handmade paper collage uses glitter paint to give the impression of fossilized stone.

2 Pansies
Wendy Beardmore
Cut-out pansies, delicately spray painted for a realistic effect, are mounted on to a printed background, in a picture adapted from Art Nouveau designs.

3 Porthole Fish
Jan Cooper
This 3D card uses mirror card to create a porthole and suspends the fish on cotton thread against a sea background.

4 Mirror Mirror
Jan Cooper
Using mirror card again, this time with a frame card supported on cork pads, and wire arms and legs for a humorous effect.

5 Prince Charming/Angel Card
Roger Riege
Cast paper is used for low relief sculpture moulded, cast and painted, then mounted on these two cards.

6 Papercast Shells
Rachel Purser
A more complex version of the starfish card (see page 80), using the same papercasting technique.

7 Ladybird

Rosalind Miller
The ladybird is printed in black and then loosely overprinted in red, with echoes of Japanese woodcuts.

8 Handmade Paper Reliefs

Penny Saxby
These two cards use treated handmade paper, washed and tinted with colour, as a background for collages of pressed flowers, fabric scraps and metal.

9 Happy Birthday

Susan Coomer
Magazine scraps, some tied with thread as parcels and one minute envelope complete with stamp, are used on a tiny scale in this unusual card.

10 Petal Paper

Olive Dean
Recycled computer paper and flowers from the designer's garden are the ingredients of this lovely paper, that is mounted on a deckle-edged background.

11 Happy Hanukkah!

Joan Hall
A humorous photomontage using magazine scraps to celebrate Hanukkah.

12 Man in the Moon

Paper Troupe
Embossed moon and stars are collaged on to a midnight background.

13 Church Wedding

Julie Dean
A paper collage using torn photocopied images, with one section mounted on card for a slightly 3D effect.

14 Paper Flower

Sophie Williams
Contrasting papers and threads are machine stitched on to a dyed paper background.

15 Teddy Bears

Mayhem Designs
These cut paper collages use a variety of brightly coloured papers for children's cards.

Apple Card
~

The concertina folds of crêpe paper in this card are easier to make than they look. Choose a fresh, apple green for the crêpe paper, and a darker green for the outer "skin".

back

METHOD

1 Make a "sandwich" with the green card at the bottom, the white card on top, and the crêpe paper in between. Draw a line down the centre of the white card, and sew the layers together along this line, green side uppermost, using backstitch and finish off leaving 3cm (1⅛in) of card and crêpe unstitched at each end.

2 Fold in half with the green card on the outside. Pencil a half apple shape on one half of the green card. Cut this out through all the layers using the craft knife and mat.

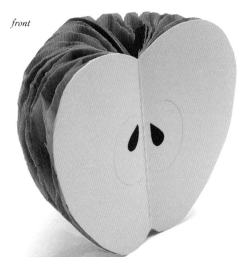

front

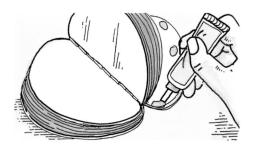

3 Open out one half of the card. Lift the bottom layer of crêpe paper off the white card and place three evenly spaced spots of glue around the edge of the white card.

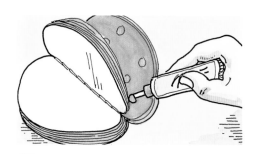

4 Press the first layer of crêpe paper on to these and allow to dry. Then glue the next layer of crêpe to the first in the same way, using only two spots of glue placed between the three spots on the first piece. Repeat with each layer of crêpe, using three and two spots of glue alternately, and gluing the last piece to the green card. Repeat the whole process on the other side.

5 Cut out two tear-drop shapes from black paper and glue these into the centre of the white card for seeds. For the core, draw two green semi-circles with a coloured pencil. Glue a black cut-out stem at the top of the apple under the crêpe paper.

Sea Monster
~

This ingenious but simple method of gluing paper circles together could be used in many different designs. This would be a good technique to teach children. Try this method for snowman Christmas cards.

METHOD

1 Cut out a wavy shape from the blue card using scissors or a craft knife.

2 For the top of the body, use scissors to cut 15 circles of each colour tissue with a 2.5cm (1in) diameter. For the centre, cut 15 circles of each colour with a 2cm (¾in) diameter. For the tail, cut 15 circles of each colour with a 1.5cm (½in) diameter.

3 To assemble each part of the body, glue alternating colour circles of tissue together. Dab four spots of glue around the edges of the circle, but put these glue spots at alternating points on the next circle and continue in this way.

4 Fold the blue card in two places, near the centre and the tail. Glue the tail over the fold, so that the tissue concertinas flat when folded. Repeat for the centre.

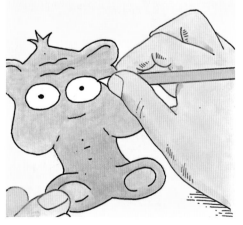

5 Make a head from green card, with white card eyes and felt tip details. Glue one end of the top body to the blue card, and the other to the back of the monster's head.

MATERIALS

Sea Monster
~

blue card, 28 × 13cm (11 × 5¼in)

•

two contrasting colours of tissue paper

•

green and white card, 10 × 7cm (4 × 2¾in)

•

felt tip pens

•

scissors or craft knife

•

cutting mat

•

fabric/paper glue

Big Mouth Hippo
~

Open this card, and this hippo will stick out his tongue at you.

MATERIALS

Big Mouth Hippo
~

piece of card, 30 × 12cm
(12 × 5in)

•

pink paper, same size as card, or
pink paint

•

white paper

•

red paper

•

black, grey and white paint

•

paintbrush

•

scissors

•

craft knife

•

cutting mat

•

ruler

•

fabric/paper glue

METHOD

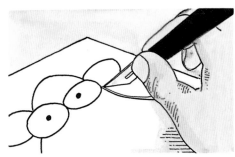

1 Fold the card in half lengthways. Draw a hippo's head on the front. Give him a great big nose and a pair of jutting-out teeth. Using a craft knife, cut around the hippo's head through both layers of card.

2 Paint the front and back of the head grey, adding the details of eyes, nostrils, ears, and outlining in black.

3 Fold the pink paper. Using the hippo head as a template, draw around it on to the pink paper. Cut out two pink paper shapes, and glue to the inside front and back of the head – or just paint the inside pink.

4 With the ruler and blunt edge of the scissors, score a line across the front of the face, about 5mm (¼in) below the eyes. Fold the lower part of the face back up from this line. Draw a pencil line along the fold, on the other half of the card.

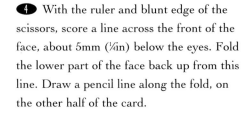

5 Cut out a tongue from the red paper. Glue it to the inside of the mouth, just above the pencil line on the back card.

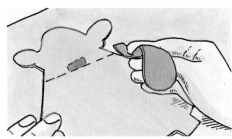

6 Spread glue on the inside of the head, as far down as the pencil line. Press the two top halves of the head together, enclosing the top of the tongue, but leaving the mouth open.

7 Paste white paper teeth inside the mouth (and on the back of the jutting teeth). Cut out a black paper epiglottis and glue in place, or paint a black epiglottis.

Loopy Lion
~

Turn the mane of this lion, and watch his expression change.

METHOD

1 Using the compass, draw two circles with a 12cm (5in) diameter, one on the white card and one on a yellow card. Make sure there is at least a 2.5cm (1in) border all around the outside of the yellow circle. Mark the centre of each circle on the back.

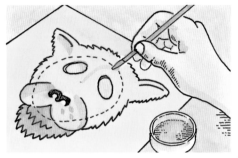

2 Cut out the white circle. Draw and paint a lion's face (without the mane) on the yellow circle, making sure that the outline of the face is just bigger than the marked circle. The eyes should be fairly large and close together, towards the top of the head. Cut out the face and make two windows for the eyes.

3 Now make the mane. Draw another circle on the other yellow card, 22cm (9in) in diameter. Draw and paint the mane, and then cut out. Pierce a small hole in the centre of the mane.

4 Glue the top of the binding pin to the centre back of the lion's head. Leave to dry, and tape over it so it won't come loose.

5 Pierce a small hole in the centre of the white circle. Glue the white circle to the mane, making sure that the holes in the centre align.

6 With the white circle uppermost, push the ends of the pin on the back of the face down through the centre of the white circle and the mane.

7 Working through the eye holes, draw different pairs of eyes, showing different expressions. Draw the first pair, then turn the mane until the eye spaces are blank again and draw the next pair, and so on until you return to the first pair. Check that all the expressions are correct and that none overlap, then take the face and move apart again. Paint in all the pairs of eyes.

8 Push the ends of the pin through the middle of the square of green card. Secure the ends with glue and, when the glue is dry, tape over to make sure that the pin is firmly attached.

9 Glue the green card square to the front of the card mount, keeping the opening on the right.

MATERIALS

Loopy Lion
~

green card mount, 52 × 26cm
(20 × 10in), scored to fold in
middle of long side

•

26 × 26cm (10 × 10in) square of
matching green card

•

2 yellow and 1 white cards,
26 × 26cm (10 × 10in)

•

watercolour, gouache or acrylic
paint for lion's eye, features and
fur

•

paintbrush

•

compass

•

binding pin with wide, flat head

•

scissors

•

craft knife

•

cutting mat

•

masking tape

•

paper glue

Starfish
~

It is easiest to use lightly or non-printed paper when first making recycled paper pulp. Photocopying or computer paper is ideal.

MATERIALS

Starfish
~

card mount scored to fold in middle
•
strong, flexible cardboard
•
paper for pulp
•
plaster of Paris
•
starfish for casting
•
plasticine
•
mixing pot and stirrer (throw-away)
•
food processor or blender
•
nylon sieve
•
scissors
•
paperclip or stapler
•
newspaper
•
tweezers
•
brush
•
metal spoon
•
absorbent cloth
•
blunt flat knife
•
wire cooling rack
•
waterproof PVA
•
all-purpose glue

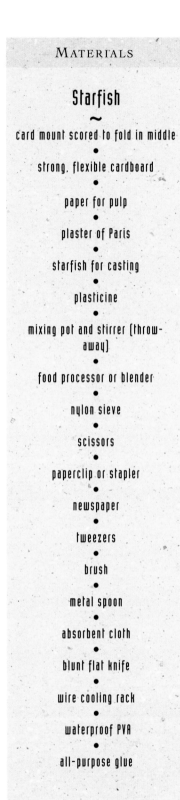

METHOD

1 Tear the paper into small pieces no bigger than 2cm (¾in) square and soak in a bowl of water for several hours. When soft, macerate the paper in a food processor or blender. Take one cup of paper and two of water at a time and blend until the fibres separate and form a "pulp". Transfer the pulp into a nylon sieve. Allow to drain but not dry out.

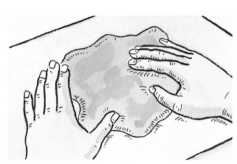

2 Warm and then press out a piece of plasticine so that it is slightly larger than the starfish. It should be about 1–2cm (⅜–¾in) thick. Gently press the starfish halfway into the surface of the plasticine.

3 Cut a strip of strong but flexible card at least 5cm (2in) taller than the height of the plasticine with the object pressed into it and large enough to tightly wrap around the plasticine, making a collar. Secure with a paperclip or staple. Place on a flat surface on newspaper.

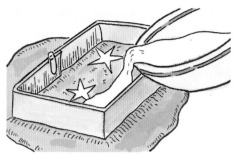

4 Mix the plaster powder to a thick, creamy consistency with water in a throw-away container, then pour carefully over the object. The tight card collar will stop the plaster escaping. (Any leaks can be checked by pressing a spare piece of plasticine against the card.) Tap the card collar to help release any air bubbles. Leave to dry and harden.

5 Remove the card collar and carefully pull off the plasticine. The object should come away. If it doesn't, release it by carefully easing or levering it out with tweezers. When the plaster casting mould is totally dry and hard, brush a very thin layer of waterproof PVA over the casting surface. Leave to dry.

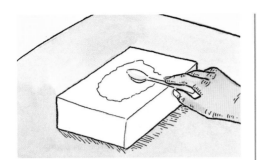

6 Spoon a small amount of the drained paper pulp on to the casting surface of the plaster mould. Using the back of a spoon press the pulp into and over the mould. Use an absorbent cloth to press down firmly on the pulp, removing all excess water and pushing the pulp into the shapes on the casting surface.

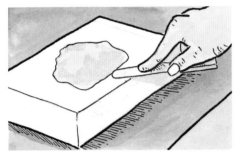

7 With a blunt, flat knife ease the paper pulp cast off and out of the plaster mould. Leave in a warm place to dry, preferably on a wire cooling rack. Mount on the card using a strong adhesive.

Windows on the World

~

This card has been made using a purchased rubber stamp. Here, the stamp has a globe design, but you could use any motif. The card is lined with white paper. It is much easier to write a message on this white lining mount, and the tissue prints look much brighter against the white background.

METHOD

1 Cut three windows in the card mount front using the craft knife and cutting mat.

2 Cut pieces of tissue paper to fit inside these windows, with a narrow border. Print the globe with white ink on to the pink and purple tissue. Print the stamp on to scrap paper until all the ink is used up and, if necessary, clean the stamp with a little water. Print the globe on to the orange paper with black ink.

3 Apply a little glue around the inside edges of the windows, carefully press down on to the tissue prints.

4 Apply a thin line of glue inside the card mount next to the fold on the right-hand side and glue the folded white paper along this line.

MATERIALS

Windows on the World
~

black card mount, 30 × 21cm [12 × 8¼in], scored to fold in middle

•

white paper, cut to the same size as the card mount and folded in middle

•

pink, purple, and orange tissue paper

•

black and white ink pads which have water-based inks

•

globe rubber stamp

•

scissors

•

craft knife

•

cutting mat

•

fabric/paper glue

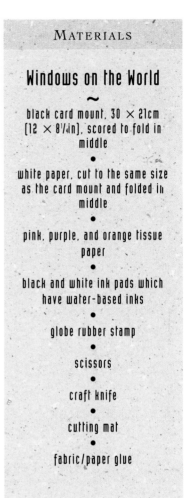

Pop-up Snowflake
~

The snowflake motif on the front of this card and the pop-up snowflake inside make a special, personal card for Christmas.

METHOD

1 Using a compass, draw a circle on one of the pieces of white paper, with a radius of 7cm (2¾in). Next, divide the circle into six segments, marking with your compass the radius around the circumference, and joining the marks through the centre with straight lines.

2 Carefully cut out the circle with scissors or a craft knife. Fold the circle in half along one line, then along the other two lines so you end up with a folded triangle shape with a curved base.

3 With the craft knife and cutting mat, cut geometric shapes within the folded triangle, making sure that you leave the two outer straight edges uncut. Unfold your "snowflake".

front

inside

4 Loosely attach the snowflake to the front of the card mount with magic tape. Place the mount on newspaper to protect the work surface, and spray from a distance of about 30cm (12in) from side to side if you want the paint even, or from the centre out if you want a graduated effect as shown here. Leave to dry, then carefully remove the snowflake stencil.

5 Glue the marbled blue paper to the inside of the mount, trimming the edges as necessary. Repeat Steps 1, 2 and 3 to make the snowflake for the inside.

6 Once you have unfolded your snowflake, take one segment, and crease the opposite way in the centre. Crease the opposite segment in the same way.

7 To attach the snowflake to the card, add two small tabs of paper measuring approximately 5 × 3mm (¼ × ⅛in) with double-sided tape, or glue. Centre the snowflake top and bottom inside the card mount. You will need to experiment to get the correct position of the snowflake depending on how flat you want it to open out. First tack one tab to the card, then close up the snowflake, then the card and press – this way you should be able to attach the snowflake evenly.

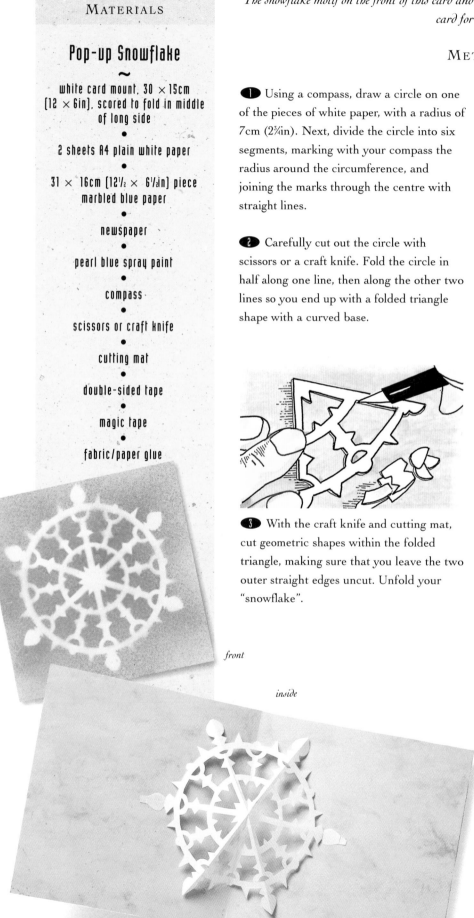

Daisy Card

~

This circular card with the flower motif looks unusual but is extremely easy to make. When cutting out the petals, avoid giving them a uniform shape. Make some slightly wider and longer than others, and arrange them in an irregular way around the heart — as they would be in their natural state.

METHOD

1 Fold the blue card in half. Using the compass, draw a 15cm (6in) circle on the folded card. Allow the circle to overlap the fold slightly on one side. Cut out the circles, making sure they are still joined along the flattened edge.

2 Cut a 5cm (2in) circle from yellow card for the heart of the flower. Lightly draw a 3cm (1¼in) circle in the middle of the blue card. Glue to the centre front of the card mount.

3 Cut individual petals from the watercolour paper, 8–10cm (3–4in) long and 1cm (½in) wide in the middle. The top edge of each petal should be straight. Dab glue at the top of each petal and press in place around the 3cm (1¼in) circle in the middle of the heart, allowing the petals to overlap each other, leaving the ends loose.

Flower Heart

~

The real flower seeds in the centre of this card are placed loose in a clear plastic bag, and move as the card is moved. Put the name of the plant inside the card, with instructions for sowing.

METHOD

1 Attach double-sided film to the front half of the brown paper. Draw a circle in the centre and draw petals radiating out from this. Cut out the petal shapes, leaving the centre uncut.

2 Carefully peel back a narrow strip of the film at the top of the card and stick this strip to the white mount, placing it accurately. Gradually peel back the film, sticking the cut-out flower to the white mount, bit by bit.

3 Cut out the centre of the flower through both layers.

4 Put the seeds into the plastic bag and tape this to the inside of the card mount so that the seeds are visible through the hole.

MATERIALS

Daisy Card

~

blue card, 36 × 18cm (14 × 7in)

•

small piece yellow card

•

watercolour paper

•

compass

•

scissors

•

paper glue

Flower Heart

~

white card mount with a textured finish, 28 × 14cm (11 × 5½in), scored to fold in middle

•

brown paper, cut to the same size as the whole card mount, front and back

•

double-sided self-adhesive film

•

seeds

•

small clear plastic bag

•

craft knife

•

cutting mat

•

sellotape

Birthday Scroll
~

This card unrolls into a cheerful birthday banner.

Birthday Scroll
~

2 white cards, 35 × 20cm
(14 × 9¹/₄in)
•
orange tissue paper, 35 × 20cm
(14 × 9¹/₄in)
•
blue tissue paper, 35 × 20cm
(14 × 9¹/₄in)
•
scrap paper
•
water-based blue paint
•
narrow satin ribbon
•
craft knife
•
cutting mat
•
iron-on adhesive
•
ruler and pencil

METHOD

1 Cover the white card with orange tissue paper using iron-on adhesive. Mark the card halfway down the long side and measure and mark each of these halves into three equal sections to make six altogether. Fold the card along these lines to form a scroll with the orange tissue on the inside.

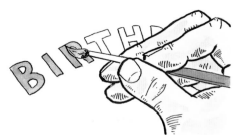

2 On the white side, on the third section from the bottom, pencil the word "happy". The base of the letters should touch the fold. Using a craft knife and cutting mat, cut round the top and sides of the letters but do not cut the bottom edge of the letters which should remain attached to the fold line. Turn the card over to the orange side and push the letters through and stand up.

3 Cut the word "birthday" from white card. Paint blue, allow to dry, and glue to the section of the orange card below the cut-out "happy".

4 Put a piece of scrap paper under the stand-up "happy" and paint the letters blue. Allow to dry. Using iron-on adhesive, glue the blue tissue to cover the white side of the card. The "shadow" of the word "happy" is now a transparent tissue window. Roll up the scroll and tie with ribbon.

Bubbly Fish
~

Pull out the tabs on the right-hand side of this fish, and watch the bubbles coming from the fish's mouth.

METHOD

1 Draw a fish shape, without a bottom jaw, on the orange card. Draw a bottom jaw with a fin on the end. Both parts should be facing right.

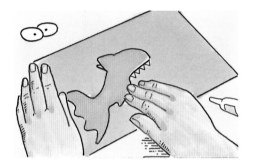

2 Cut out teeth from the white card, and glue to the top and bottom jaws. Glue the main body of the fish to the left-hand side of the blue card. Glue on a pair of eyes, marking the pupils with the felt pen.

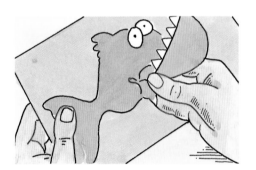

3 Using a strong glue, attach the binding pin to the back of the bottom jaw, behind the fin. Push the pin through the body of the fish and the card, so that the jaw swings from the fin. Fold the pin legs out behind the card.

4 Using the craft knife and ruler, cut three pairs of vertical slots on the blue card to the right of the fish.

5 Cut three strips of blue card to slide between the slots. They should be slightly narrower than each pair of slots, and long enough to reach from the right-hand edge of the card to the middle.

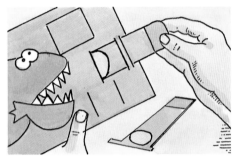

6 Cut out three circles of white paper, and glue these to the left-hand end of the strips. Cut three tabs of orange card, and glue these to the other end of the strips. Slide the strips into the slots.

7 Glue another piece of blue card as a backing to the main card. Do not attach it on the right-hand edge and take great care not to get any glue on to the slots or the strips of card, or you won't be able to slide the strips in and out.

MATERIALS

Bubbly Fish
~

3 sheets of blue card, 30 × 21cm
(12 × 8¼in)
•
1 sheet of orange card, 30 × 21cm
(12 × 8¼in)
•
sheet of white paper or thin card
•
binding pin with wide, flat head
•
pencil and felt-tip pen
•
scissors
•
craft knife
•
cutting mat
•
ruler
•
all-purpose adhesive
•
fabric/paper glue

Introduction

Throughout history pictures have been made using fabric and stitchery. The ancient Egyptians used appliqué and, in past centuries in the West, girls as young as five stitched their first samplers. There are all kinds of techniques to explore whether you are an experienced dressmaker or embroiderer or have never stitched in your life. In the latter case, follow the simple instructions or make the cards using glue.

Felt is easy and fun because it doesn't fray while, by fraying silk, you can create a beautiful background. Visit and enjoy the magic of fabric shops and haberdashers with a new eye for detail — perception changes when you need such small quantities and you can buy the best. You can use fabrics

Fanciful Fabric

right across the range from hand-embroidered silk to vividly coloured man-made fabric. Alternatively, rummage in scrap bags for remnants, buttons and ribbons. Explore craft museums and look through library books for examples of exquisite antique quilts, patchwork and embroidery and collect pictures of borders, colour combinations and motifs to act as an inspiration for your cards.

Felt Cornucopia
~

The vibrant colours and bold shapes are what first strike the eye on this card. The addition of embroidery stitches, however, is a vital part of this design, providing depth and detail.

MATERIALS

Felt Cornucopia
~

card mount, 28 × 18cm (11 × 7in), scored to fold in middle
•
tracing paper
•
plain white or pastel felt for background, 18 × 14cm (7 × 5½in)
•
small pieces of felt in various colours
•
embroidery threads in several colours
•
embroidery needle
•
scissors
•
double-sided tape or fabric glue

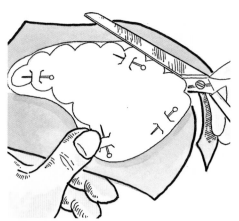

1 Draw the cornucopia on to tracing paper and cut out the shapes. Use these in turn as a guide to cut out the cornucopia, leaves, stems, fruit and flowers from the coloured felt pieces.

METHOD

2 Glue the cornucopia on to the background felt, and assemble the other pieces, gluing each in turn. Pieces that lie behind other pieces, such as the stems behind the fruit, should be stuck down first.

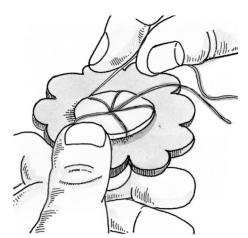

3 Add detail to the leaves and outline the main shapes with simple embroidery stitches, using three strands of thread and contrasting colours.

4 Stick the finished picture to the front of the mount either with double-side tape, or with fabric glue applied thinly.

Variation
Try other shapes in your felt collage. An arrangement of shells would work well, for example.

Window with Lace Curtains
~

This card uses a mixture of patterned and plain fabrics and simple embroidery to give an interesting effect.

METHOD

1 Iron flowered fabric on to iron-on adhesive. Cut around the flower shapes. Remove paper backing of web, and iron floral fabric on to one of the plain fabrics.

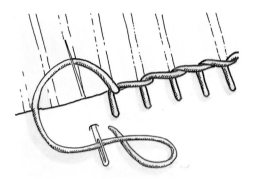

2 Fold over and iron a hem at the top of both pieces of plain fabric. Lay the plain fabric behind the fabric with the flowers, and the striped fabric behind this. Pin these layers together. Sew blanket stitch over the two joins with the cream thread.

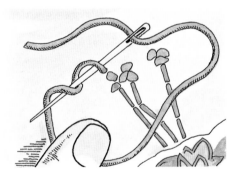

3 Using green embroidery thread and back stitch, sew on flower stems. With pink and blue thread, sew large French knots to look like flower buds, and sew petals in lazy daisy stitch. Sew two birds in the sky with grey thread and back stitch. Make sure that these embroidered features will all fit within the window mount.

4 Place a strip of lace each side of the picture and tack lightly at top and bottom. Apply glue to the inside edges of the window mount, and press down in place over the picture.

5 Glue the backing to the window mount. Glue on the two bows.

MATERIALS

Window with Lace Curtains
~

three-panel cream blank card mount with cut-out window, with 17.5 × 12.5cm (6¾ × 5in) front

•

2 plain, 1 striped and 1 flowered pieces of fabric

•

iron-on adhesive

•

2cm-wide (1in) lace strips

•

2 purchased cream satin bows (or make your own)

•

green, pink, blue, grey and cream embroidery thread

•

embroidery needle

•

scissors

•

fabric/paper glue

Quilted House

~

This is a house-moving card in a quilted frame. If you are sending it to someone you know well, perhaps you could add extra appliquéd details relating to their family or new home.

MATERIALS

Quilted House

~

card mount, 29 × 17cm
(11½ × 6¾in), scored to fold in middle

•

rectangle of thin card fractionally smaller than front of mount

•

plain peach-coloured fabric

•

calico

•

patterned fabric

•

thin wadding

•

iron-on adhesive and iron

•

narrow peach-coloured satin ribbon

•

2 purchased bows to match ribbon

•

thread to match patterned fabric

•

needle and thread, or sewing machine

•

scissors

•

pinking shears (optional)

•

craft knife

•

cutting mat

•

fabric/paper glue

METHOD

1 Cut a piece of calico slightly smaller than the backing card, and glue this to the card at the edges.

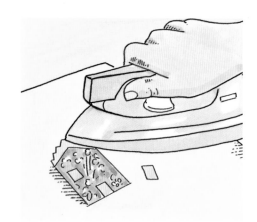

2 Cut out a house from the patterned fabric and a roof and windows from the peach. Fix to the centre of the calico using iron-on adhesive. Frame with four strips of ribbon, glued lightly in place.

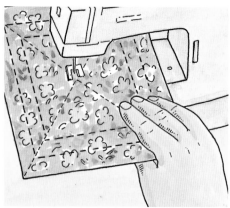

3 Cut a piece of patterned fabric about 2.5cm (1in) bigger than the backing card. Sandwich a piece of wadding between this and a similar-sized piece of calico. Stitch across this in lines to make a quilt. Stitch diagonal lines from each corner. Cut a square from the centre of the quilted fabric and turn a hem under so that the quilting frames the house and ribbons. Glue the quilted frame over the calico, folding the quilting over on to the back of the backing card, and gluing the edges.

4 Cut other small shapes from the plain peach fabric and from the patterned fabric, and iron these on to the frame in the same way as before.

5 Glue the two small bows to the frame.

6 Glue the quilted picture to the front of the card mount.

Scented Heart
~

If you do not want the card to look bare when the scented heart is removed, add another motif beneath it.

METHOD

1 Cover the rectangle of thin card with the fabric, folding this behind the card and securing it with glue or sellotape.

2 Sew on a border of lace around the edges of the card, pleating it at the corners. Sew on a cream bow at each corner.

3 Make a loop of ribbon and sew one end of this to the back of the padded heart and the other end to the back of the blue bow. Sew the blue bow to the fabric-covered card, so that the heart hangs just below the centre of the mount.

4 Glue the finished collage on to the front of your card mount.

5 If using, sew or glue a lace heart or other motif to the fabric where it will be covered by the padded heart.

MATERIALS

Scented Heart
~

card mount, 30 × 21cm (12 × 8¼in), scored to fold in middle

•

thin card, the same size as the front of the mount

•

fabric to cover thin card

•

purchased lavender bag heart

•

purchased lace heart or other motif to go under padded heart (optional)

•

lace trimming

•

4 cream bows

•

blue bow

•

narrow satin ribbon to match blue bow

•

needle and thread

•

scissors

•

craft knife

•

cutting mat

•

masking tape or sellotape

•

fabric/paper glue

Teddy in the Window

~

The attractive feature of this card is that the teddy, preferably filled with lavender or potpourri, can be removed from the card. You could include a small, appliquéd motif under the teddy, so that if it was removed the card would still make a picture.

MATERIALS

Teddy in the Window
~

36 × 21cm (12½ × 8¼in) thick card mount, scored to fold in middle

•

25 × 21cm (10 × 8¼in) calico for background and window

•

27 × 22cm (10¾ × 8¾in) plain blue fabric for border

•

scrap of green striped fabric for bear

•

15.5 × 10.5cm (6 × 4in) blue-striped fabric for house

•

potpourri or cotton wool

•

scrap of lace trimming

•

embroidered flowers trimming

•

blue ribbon

•

3 pearl, 2 blue buttons

•

iron-on adhesive

•

blue, cream and green sewing and embroidery threads

•

needle and embroidery needles

•

scissors

•

craft knife

•

cutting mat

•

fabric/paper glue

METHOD

1 Cut calico to fit mount for background. Pin on blue-striped fabric turning edges under. Sew fabric in place using back stitch and blue thread.

2 Iron adhesive on to a small piece of calico. Draw house shape. Cut out and iron this on to striped fabric.

3 Sew on the buttons and embroider green leaves around two lower buttons. Sew a border around the edge of the house with cream embroidery thread.

4 Place whole calico house and backing into centre of large piece of blue fabric. Fold edges of blue fabric inwards over calico, turning to form a hem, and sew in place with blue thread.

5 With embroidery thread, sew blue french knots at 3cm (1¼in) intervals. Sew two green knots at the top corners, and one each at the bottom. Using green thread, sew two lines of back stitch at top of picture.

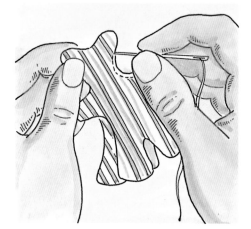

6 Cut out two matching pieces of fabric for the front and back of the bear. With cream sewing thread, sew the right sides together, leaving an opening at the top of the head. Turn inside out, and fill with either potpourri or cotton wool. Slip-stitch opening in head. Trim neck with lace and flowers, and embroider eyes.

7 Sew a loop of blue ribbon to the bear with blue sewing thread.

8 When all sewing is complete, glue to the front of the card mount. Hang the bear from the central button at the top.

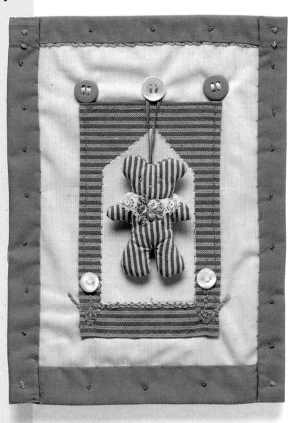

Calico Cat
~

Think of ways to personalize this card for a special event. For a child's birthday, you could use dressmaking scraps from their favourite clothes, or do an appliqué picture of the family pet. For a mother's birthday – perhaps an appliqué picture of her favourite flowers, or a "portrait" of her home.

METHOD

1 Cut sixteen 5cm (2in) squares from the patterned fabrics and stitch together to form a block of four rows, with four squares in each row. Press.

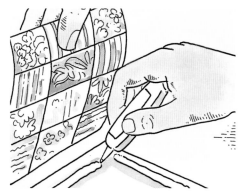

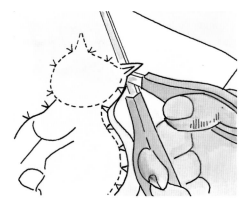

2 Transfer the cat template (see p125) and stitching lines on to the calico using dressmaker's carbon. Cut out, allowing an extra 5mm (¼in). Clip 'V'-shapes of excess seam allowance and press under.

4 Carefully glue the patchwork to the front of the folded card mount. Stick a length of tape along each side to conceal the raw edges. This can be hand stitched or secured with a wide machine stitch in matching thread. Sew a button on to each corner with brown embroidery thread and glue to the mount.

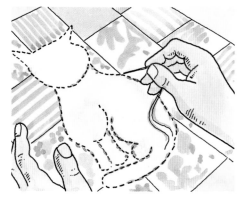

3 Slip-stitch the cat on to the patchwork square with white sewing cotton. With brown embroidery thread, sew a decorative small running stitch over the stitching lines. Sew the whiskers so that they overlap on to the patchwork, and sew the nose in satin stitch. Work the eyes in green satin stitch. Press lightly.

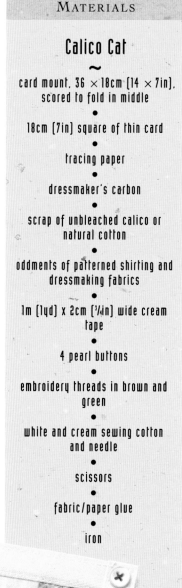

MATERIALS

Calico Cat
~
card mount, 36 × 18cm (14 × 7in), scored to fold in middle
•
18cm (7in) square of thin card
•
tracing paper
•
dressmaker's carbon
•
scrap of unbleached calico or natural cotton
•
oddments of patterned shirting and dressmaking fabrics
•
1m (1yd) x 2cm (¾in) wide cream tape
•
4 pearl buttons
•
embroidery threads in brown and green
•
white and cream sewing cotton and needle
•
scissors
•
fabric/paper glue
•
iron

Folk Art Angel
~

This angel could be made into a double-sided mobile or Christmas decoration by covering the reverse side to match the front and attaching a hanging loop of cord halfway along the back.

MATERIALS

Folk Art Angel
~

thin white card, 30 × 15cm
(12 × 6in)
•
tracing paper
•
20 × 10cm (8 × 4in) piece of
printed cotton lawn
•
18 × 8cm (7 × 3in) piece of black
felt
•
small scrap of pale orange felt
•
iron-on fusible bonding
•
black felt-tip pen
•
scissors
•
iron

METHOD

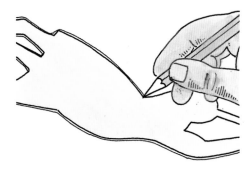

1 Trace the angel template (see p124) on to tracing paper, transferring all the markings. Trace the main silhouette on to thin card and cut out carefully.

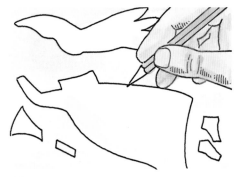

2 Reverse the tracing so that the angel now faces towards the left and trace the individual outlines for the dress, hair, shoes and trumpet directly on to iron-on fusible bonding. Cut out each shape roughly.

3 Following the manufacturer's instructions, iron the dress shape on to the reverse side of the printed fabric. Iron the hair and shoe patterns on to the black felt and the two sections of the trumpet on to the pale orange felt in the same way. Cut out all six pieces accurately around the pencil lines, and remove the backing papers.

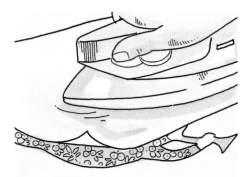

4 Place the dress shape on to the angel cut-out, carefully aligning the edges and, using a cloth to protect the surface, fix in place with a cool iron. Attach the felt pieces in the same way, then draw in the eye with a fine felt-tip pen.

Rabbit and Ribbons

~

Here is another way to use ribbons. This would make an attractive "new baby" card.

METHOD

1 Cut white card to approximately 14 × 11cm (6 × 4½in). Cut window mount in centre 7½ × 5cm (3 × 2in).

2 Using glue or double-sided sellotape, place decorative ribbon around edge of the white card.

3 Cut rabbit shape from both blue card and cotton wool. Place satin ribbon under cut-out card with the wool rabbit beneath. Fix with masking tape, sew nose and eye with black thread. Glue rabbit card to white mount.

4 Glue on tail. Glue broderie anglaise around the edge of the ribbon.

5 Mount on to blue card, and finally stick the pink bow at the top left-hand corner.

Cat with Tartan Ribbon

~

A fabric stiffener has been used to make this cat, but you could use flocked paper, or flocking powder, available at craft shops.

METHOD

1 Glue a strip of the middle-sized ribbon across the mount to form the wall.

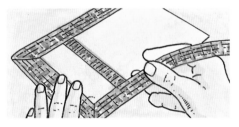

2 Glue a border of the widest tartan ribbon around the edges of the mount, pleating it at the corners.

3 Draw and cut out a cat shape from the fabric stiffener. If you use flocking powder, apply glue to a cat shape made from paper, sprinkle on the powder and leave to dry.

4 Make the two narrower size bows from the ribbons. Glue the cat, bows and beads to the card. Use beads for the cat's eye and nose.

MATERIALS

Cat with Tartan Ribbon

~

card mount, 26 × 16.5cm [10¼ × 6¼in], scored to fold in middle

•

black fabric stiffener or paper and flocking powder

•

bugle beads in different sizes

•

3 widths of tartan ribbon — 17mm [⅔in], 10mm [⅓in], 5mm [⅕in]

•

scissors

•

PVA glue

Rabbit and Ribbons

~

blue and white cards, 31 × 18cm [12¼ × 7in]

•

cotton wool or wadding

•

10cm [4in] white satin ribbon, 4cm [1½in] wide

•

70cm [30in] decorative ribbon

•

1m [1yd] white broderie anglaise

•

1 pink satin bow

•

black thread

•

masking tape and PVA glue

•

craft knife and cutting mat

•

PVA glue

MATERIALS

Homespun Star
~

30 × 15cm (12 × 6in) card mount, scored to fold in middle

•

15cm (6in) squares of thin card

•

tracing paper

•

scraps of different ginghams, and red sewing cotton

•

20cm (8in) square of main fabric

•

scissors

•

masking tape

•

fabric/paper glue

Flower in Organza
~

blue card mount, 21 × 15cm (8¼ × 6in), scored to fold in middle

•

pieces of pink silk and silk organza

•

small blue silk flower

•

fine silver thread

•

scissors

•

craft knife

•

cutting mat

•

fabric glue

•

iron-on adhesive (optional)

Homespun Star
~

Made with scraps of gold and silver fabrics and ribbons, this would also make an unusual Christmas card.

METHOD

1 Trace the star design from the template (see page 124) and number each separate piece. Using these as a guide, cut out five triangles and one pentagon from gingham.

2 Cut out a circle 10cm (4in) in diameter, from a light-coloured gingham. Using fabric glue, stick the pieces down on to this to form a star.

3 Glue the circle to the centre of the main fabric, and work a zigzag stitch by hand or machine to cover the raw edges. Stretch the finished piece over the square of card, folding the edges behind the card, and stick down with masking tape. Glue to the front of the card mount.

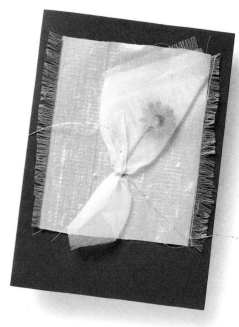

Flower in Organza
~

For a special event, write a message on paper and stain with diluted instant coffee so that it looks like a scrap of parchment.

METHOD

1 Cut a rectangle of silk to fit within the front of the card mount. Fray the silk on two edges.

2 Cut a square of organza in proportion to the size of the flower. Fray the top edge.

3 Wrap the organza round the flower to make a small "bouquet" (the flower should point to one corner of the organza). Tie with thread.

4 Glue the silk to the card mount, applying the glue very thinly or it will stain the silk. As an alternative, use iron-on adhesive.

5 Glue the bouquet to the silk, applying glue only on the thread behind the bow – again do not glue this anywhere else or it will stain the fabric.

Flower Print Vase
~

You will need one plain and two floral-print fabrics for this card. The flowers in one print should be separate enough to cut out, and the background colour of this fabric should be the same as the plain fabric (in this case, plain calico). The iron-on adhesive used to make the fabric adhere should also prevent it fraying.

METHOD

1 Iron the two floral fabrics on to the adhesive, carefully following the manufacturer's instructions.

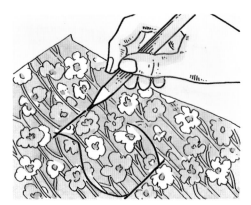

2 Draw a vase shape on the fabric with the smaller print, and cut out. Cut out single flowers from the other floral fabric.

4 Apply glue to the inside edge of the frame and lay it over the picture, making sure the fabric is stretched flat.

5 Glue the frame on to the front of the card mount.

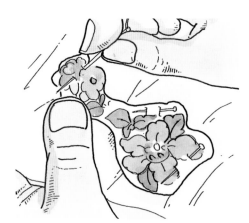

3 Remove the paper backing from the iron-on adhesive, and pin these shapes to the plain fabric background. Press with an iron, according to the manufacturer's instructions. Measure around the vase and flowers, and cut a frame to fit around them from the card.

MATERIALS

Flower Print Vase
~

card mount, 32 × 21cm
(12½ × 8¼in), scored to fold
in middle

•

card for frame, same size as front
of mount

•

fabric pen

•

2 floral print fabrics

•

calico, or other plain fabric

•

iron-on adhesive

•

scissors

•

ruler

•

craft knife

•

cutting mat

•

pins

•

fabric/paper glue

Gallery

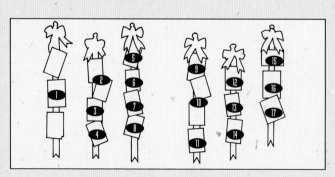

1 Whale/Heart/Crown
Tanya Marsh
Felt, fur fabric and velvet appliquéd images are machine-appliquéd on to hessian. The inspiration for these cards came from an exhibition of African hand-appliquéd flags.

2 Tartan Heart/Tartan Flower
Thérèse McDermott
A pressed flower and a tartan heart are mounted on fabric and covered with printed acetate.

3 Pink Bouquet
Andrea Liss
Dried flowers, ribbons, lace, tissue and a brass charm bow make up an intriguing 3D card.

4 Gold Leaf Heart
Kate Twelvetrees
Silk with seed pearls is the background for a gold leaf heart wrapped in silk organza and tied with silver thread.

5 Tartan Tree
Sally Norris
Two tartan appliquéd fabrics form this jolly Christmas tree that is machine stitched on to textured paper.

6 Country Bouquet
Andrea Liss
Layers of frayed fabric are the background for a simple bunch of dried flowers tied with satin ribbon.

7 **Silk Flowers**

Sophie Williams
These flowers are machine embroidered on to silk.

8 **Golden Cherub**

Andrea Liss
Lace, fabric and paper are the background for this foil cherub.

9 **Heart and Sole**

Ingrid Duffy
This card uses appliquéd patterned fabric, a stitched-on bead eye and embroidery on a calico background. The heart is painted on.

10 **Sunglasses Fish/Hearts and Flowers**

Jilly Marcuson
These hand-painted silk images use gold gutta in the same way as the card on page 101.

11 **Felt Flower**

Rebecca Salmon
This hand-stitched felt appliqué card uses simple colour and outlines.

12 **African Man**

Susan Phrakhun
This machine-stitched collage with dried flowers and hand-printed figure is inspired by the primitive art of Africa.

13 **Magic Mirror**

Kate Twelvetrees
Four layers of frayed silk form a background for a tiny mirror.

14 **Flight to Freedom**

Kate Twelvetrees
Frayed silk and a gold net "cage" create the scene for the photocopied escaping bird, tinted with gold paint.

15 **Golden Crown**

Sophie Williams
A fake fur background holds a gold, machine-appliquéd crown with stitched colour details.

16 **Woolly Sheep**

Ingrid Duffy
Denim, sheep's wool and felt make up a touch-freely card! There is also an inked frame and title.

17 **Furry Piggy**

Cluck
Fake fur completely covers the back and the front of this card except for the window revealing a drawn pig.

Abstract Silk Painting
~

Silk gives a special, rich feeling to a card. The gutta used as a masking medium is like glue and stops the colours running into each other.

MATERIALS

Abstract Silk Painting
~

card mount, 34 × 17cm (13½ × 6¾in), scored to fold in middle
•
card for frame, same size as front of card mount
•
several pieces of paper, larger than card
•
piece of silk, same size as front of mount
•
different-coloured silk dyes
•
gutta
•
medium-sized paintbrush
•
gutta dispenser (pen)
•
scissors
•
craft knife
•
cutting mat
•
ruler
•
pins or masking tape
•
fabric/paper glue
•
iron

METHOD

1 Cut a frame for your design from the framing card.

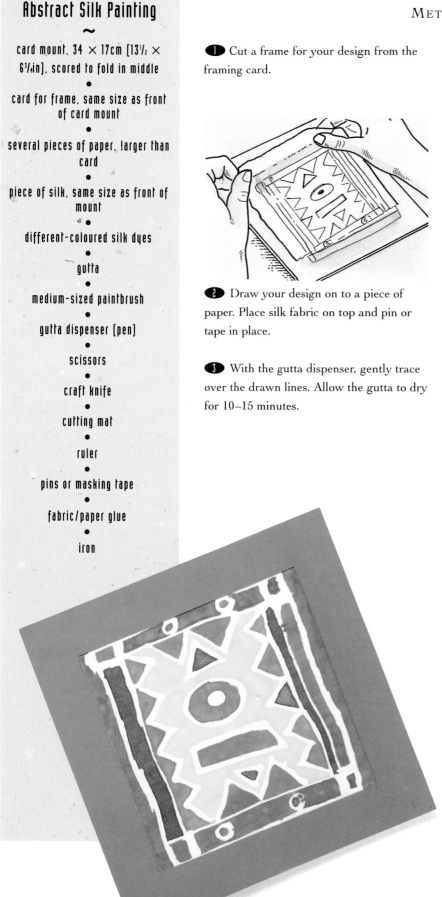

2 Draw your design on to a piece of paper. Place silk fabric on top and pin or tape in place.

3 With the gutta dispenser, gently trace over the drawn lines. Allow the gutta to dry for 10–15 minutes.

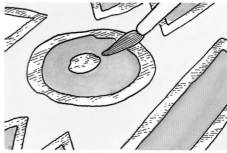

4 Dip the paintbrush into the dye. Slowly fill in the shapes by pressing the tip of the brush on to the centre of the area to be painted, and allowing the colour to spread. Take care not to flood the silk. The gutta will keep the colours separate as long as there is not too much dye on the brush.

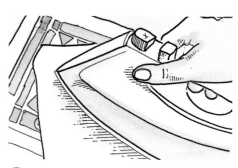

5 Allow the dye to dry. Cover design with a clean piece of paper and fix the silk dye by holding an iron on the design according to the manufacturer's instructions.

6 Wash the gutta out with cold water, and iron the design again between two sheets of clean paper.

7 Place the frame over the design and cut out the print. Spread glue along the inside edge of the frame. Lay it over the print, and glue to front of card mount, taking care not to get glue on silk.

Variation
This card has a simple card window mount, but for a special occasion try making a padded silk frame, using a card base, wadding, and a toning piece of plain silk.

Silk Painted Card
~

The gutta acts as a barrier which helps to contain the colours, preventing one from bleeding into another. Usually the gutta is removed by washing, but in this case a gold metallic gutta has been used and this has been left to form part of the design.

METHOD

1 Wash and dry silk and stretch it on to the frame, using double-sided tape or map pins. Make sure it is very tightly stretched.

2 Using a textile pen, draw your design on to the silk. (If you make a mistake, you can wash out the pen marks.) Alternatively, draw the design on to a piece of paper as in the method used for Abstract Silk Painting (opposite).

3 Using a continuous, strong line of gutta, go over the lines of your drawing, pressing and squeezing the tube at the same time to achieve this. Use the gutta to draw a box edge around the whole design.

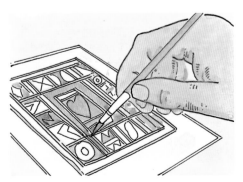

4 Prepare the colours according to the manufacturer's instructions and paint the design, using the tip of the paintbrush. The colour will spread to the gutta edges, so there is no need to use heavy brush-strokes.

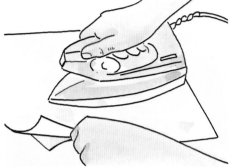

5 When the painting is complete, remove the design from the frame and iron it on the reverse side to fix the colours, using a silk setting. Cover the design with cloth or paper and rotate the iron for about 5 minutes.

6 Cut the design out, next to the gold gutta frame. This prevents fraying. Attach your design to the front of the card mount with double-sided tape or iron-on adhesive.

MATERIALS

Silk Painted Card
~
card mount, 21 × 15cm [8¼ × 6in], scored to fold in middle
•
medium-weight white silk
•
iron and cloth or paper for ironing
•
gold metallic gutta
•
silk paint colours
•
textile pen
•
paintbrush
•
frame [from a craft shop, or use an old picture frame]
•
scissors
•
double-sided tape or map pins
•
iron-on adhesive or double-sided tape

Glittery Bird

~

This card has been designed to hang up and is on flat card rather than a folded mount.

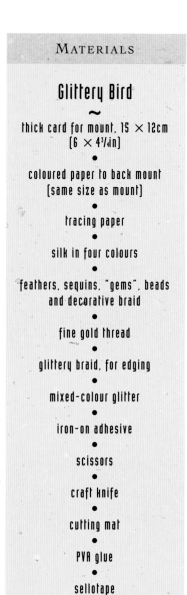

METHOD

1 Iron a piece of silk large enough for your bird on to the adhesive. Cut out the shape of the bird (you could draw the shape on paper first and lay this on the silk as a template).

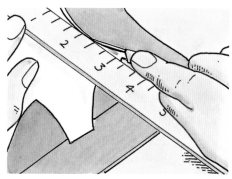

2 Lay the bird on the card and draw round it. Cut out a rectangle of card around the outline of the bird, but cut it just short of the beak and tail, so that these shapes project beyond the rectangle.

3 Cut out small pieces of silk for the wing and beak details and iron these on in the same way. Draw a line of glue round the edge of the bird with a fine point, and glue the gold thread to this to make an outline.

4 Apply PVA glue to the rest of the card and sprinkle this with the glitter. Shake off the excess.

5 Use PVA glue to attach all the feathers, beads, sequins, strips of braid etc. Draw a line of glue around the edge of the card and glue on the glittery braid.

6 Use the tape to attach a loop of gold thread to the back of the card. Cover the back of the card with a piece of coloured paper cut to the correct size. The finished card may be hung from the loop of gold thread.

Cross-stitch Heart

~

Try this design, embroidered in simple cross-stitch, for a card with an old-fashioned, Victorian flavour.

METHOD

1 Using four strands of thread and following the diagram on p123, work the heart and bow on to the Aida cloth in cross-stitch, ensuring that all the stitches lie in the same direction. Press lightly from the back.

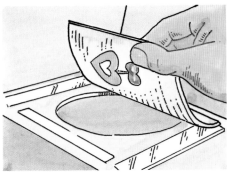

2 Stick lengths of double-sided tape around the reverse of the card's oval opening. Cut the embroidery to size so that it is 5mm (¼in) smaller on each side than the card itself. Peel off the backing and carefully stick the Aida cloth face down into place, so that it is central within the oval.

3 Fold the card flap over to cover the back of the embroidery and secure with more double-sided tape.

Variation
You could create a design of your own – perhaps an initial. Simply draw the outline on graph paper and fill in with pen each square which the line crosses. Use this as your pattern.

Felt Collage

~

Before you cut out the pieces for your collage, sketch a few designs on paper until you have created one you like. This card has been designed with a twenty-first birthday in mind.

METHOD

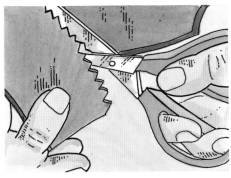

1 Cut out various shapes from felt using decorative and straight-edge scissors. You should have a larger piece for the background, and a variety of motifs to make up the design.

2 Arrange the pieces to achieve the best design. Glue the pieces in place.

3 Glue the finished collage to the front of the card mount.

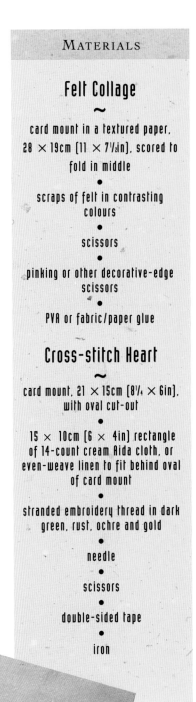

For Your
Wedding

Introduction

Of course all the cards in this book are a labour of love but the cards in this section involve perhaps something a little extra or different. In some cases, such as the complex and delicate quilling cards, this is a meticulous new technique to learn and apply. Sometimes, the cards are evocative of another era. In other cases, what makes them so extra special is the involvement of family or friends to create unique collections of memories. These are particularly pleasing because the gift of time and attention extends beyond the maker and can be particularly touching mementoes. Some of the cards have gifts to remove and use separately, and some are particularly unusual or decorative. One is

Labour of Love

in a highly decorated book form and another is not, strictly speaking, a card at all. The very best thing about making your own cards is that they can be totally unique, completely personal both to the giver and recipient. Explore this avenue of possibilities with your imagination.

Ribbon Rose Bouquet
~

Make this romantic bouquet from a few lengths of ribbon, a small piece of silk, and some decorative lace edging.

MATERIALS

Ribbon Rose Bouquet
~

card mount, 20 × 40cm (8 × 16in), scored to fold in middle of long side

•

9cm (3½in) circle of thin card

•

13cm (5in) circle of dark pink silk or satin

•

small amount of polyester wadding

•

60 x 8cm (24 x 3in) cream lace edging

•

short lengths of green, pink, bronze and cream satin ribbons in various widths

•

needle and thread

•

scissors

•

craft knife

•

cutting mat

•

fabric/paper glue

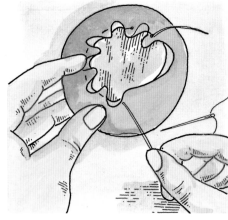

METHOD

1 Make several ribbon roses in different colours and widths, reserving narrow and green ribbons for Step 4. To do this, fold the ribbon at a right angle, two-thirds along its length, then fold as in the illustration above. When you reach the end of your ribbon, use your fingers to open out the centre of your rose into a rounded flower. Make several stab stitches through the base of the rose to hold the ribbon in place.

2 Cut a circle of wadding the same size as the card circle, and glue the wadding to the card. Gather the edge of the pink silk or satin circle to fit over the card and wadding, and slip-stitch in place.

3 Neatly join the two ends of the lace, and gather to fit the circle. Sew in place, adjusting the folds.

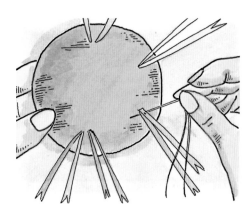

4 Sew a few streamers of narrow ribbon to the padded circle. Then sew or glue on loops of green ribbon "leaves", and the ribbon roses.

5 Use fabric glue to fix the bouquet to the front of the card mount.

Wedding Veil

~

Write a "secret" message under the lace, before tying the handkerchief to the card, to be discovered when the handkerchief is removed.

METHOD

1 Cut heart shapes from the thin card. Apply a thin layer of glue to one side and press the hearts on to the gold leaf. Leave to dry, and then lift them off carefully. The gold leaf will have adhered to the hearts, with loose pieces around the edges: fold these behind the hearts. Alternatively, paint the hearts gold.

2 Cover the card rectangle with the paper, folding it over the edges and gluing behind the card.

3 Gather the handkerchief together near the top and, holding it between your fingers, position it on the card. Mark the card on either side of the gathering, close to the fabric.

4 Remove the handkerchief and make small holes at the points marked. Pass the ribbon through the holes from the back and tie round the handkerchief, making a bow. Allow plenty of ribbon so that the hanging ends are long.

5 Glue the hearts to the card, and the card to the front of the mount.

Paper Lace Valentine

~

Printed scraps were used by Victorians to decorate screens and for many other purposes – a technique known as "decoupage".

METHOD

1 Cut a rectangular shape from a white paper doily. Cut out individual motifs such as hearts or flowers from the other doilies, looking for interesting shapes.

2 Draw around the outside of the doily shape on to the coloured paper, marking where some of the holes in the "lace" are. Cut out the coloured paper and glue the doily on to the paper shape.

3 Glue the doily to the mount to leave a small card border all the way round.

4 Use your imagination to decorate the card in elaborate Victorian style with cut-out scraps and motifs from the other doilies. Gold and silver foil are especially effective.

MATERIALS

Wedding Veil

~

cream card mount, 30 × 17cm (12 × 6³⁄₄in), scored to fold in middle

•

thin card for hearts

•

rectangle of thin card same size as the front of mount

•

decorative background paper

•

handkerchief, as lacy as possible

•

thin blue ribbon

•

mock gold leaf transfer sheet, or gold paint

•

scissors

•

fabric/paper glue

Paper Lace Valentine

~

coloured card for mount, 32 × 21cm (12¹⁄₂ × 8¹⁄₄in), scored and folded in middle

•

coloured paper for backing doily

•

paper doilies in white, gold and silver

•

reproduction Victorian scraps

•

sharp scissors

•

craft knife

•

cutting mat

•

paper glue

Ribbon Frame Card

~

You could buy a clip frame and a greetings card box from a craft shop, make the mount to fit the frame and send the card and frame together. The roses on this card are not attached to the ribbon so that they can be easily removed, tucked into the clip frame, glued to the glass or hung from the frame with ribbon. To make the deckle edge of the card mount, rip the edge along a ruler, or use craft scissors designed for this purpose. When gluing on the ribbon, avoid using too much glue or it will stain the ribbon. Choose a good fabric glue that will allow you to rub off the excess when dry.

MATERIALS

Ribbon Frame Card

~

card mount, 26 × 18cm (10¼ × 7in), made from thick watercolour paper with a deckle edge, scored to fold in middle

•

clip frame, same size as front of card mount (optional)

•

backing fabric, slightly smaller than front of card mount

•

black and white family photograph, or a laser copy reduced to suitable size

•

4 small dried roses or silk flowers

•

narrow ribbon, approximately 1cm (⅜in) wide, to frame the photograph and cross over (or plait three lengths of narrow ribbon)

•

scissors

•

fabric/paper glue

METHOD

1 Glue the backing fabric to the card mount, then glue the photo in place on top of the fabric.

2 Apply a thin line of glue running from the centre of the bottom edge of the photo to one bottom corner. Lay the ribbon on to this with a loose end of ribbon at the centre bottom of the photo. Wait a few minutes until it is dry.

3 Apply a line of glue along the adjacent vertical edge of the photo. Turn the ribbon and lay it along this line of glue, leaving a small pleat of ribbon at the corner of the photo. Again, wait until dry.

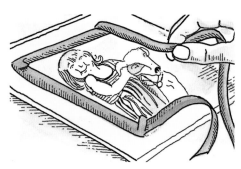

4 Glue the ribbon along the remaining two and a half sides of the photo in the same way, leaving a small open pleat at each corner and a second loose end in the centre bottom edge of the photograph.

5 Cross over the ends of the ribbon at the bottom centre and glue down the ends. If you are using narrow satin ribbon, make it into a bow.

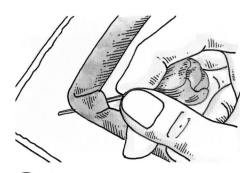

6 Thread the stems of the roses through the open pleats in the corners.

Family Flowers

~

This card can be used for a variety of special occasions – for an anniversary, a thank you card from a family, a bon voyage card from a group of friends, or a really large bouquet of mixed flowers for a great-grandparent's birthday. For this card, flat, open flowers with large centres work best.

METHOD

1 Remove the flower heads from the stems and cut off any remaining stem as close to the back of the flower head as possible. Glue the flower heads to the background paper and glue the photographs to the flower centres.

4 Lay the picture on the cream card mount and mark this so you have a narrow border. Carefully mount the picture, applying glue to the card rather than the picture itself.

MATERIALS

Family Flowers

~

cream card for mount, 24 × 24cm (9½ × 9½in), scored and folded in centre

•

coloured paper for background, same size as front of mount

•

small cut-out faces from photographs to fit flower centres

•

silk flowers

•

wide ribbon in organza or similar fabric

•

scissors

•

craft knife

•

cutting mat

•

PVA glue

2 Cut the stems to an appropriate length and arrange these under the edges of the flowers to look as though they come from the flower centres.

3 Lay a long piece of ribbon across the card and attach the centre to the card with a dab of glue. Glue the stems in place over the ribbon. When dry, tie the ribbon round the stems in a bow.

Autographed Hearts
~

Break the wax seal to reveal the messages in this heart-shaped book. This is an ideal card to send from several members of a group – a colleague's leaving card, for instance.

MATERIALS

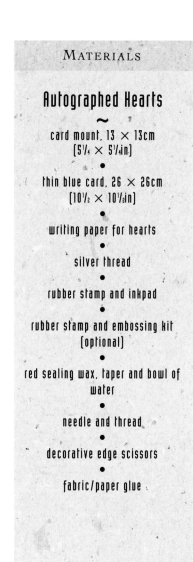

Autographed Hearts
~

card mount, 13 × 13cm
[5¼ × 5¼in]
•
thin blue card, 26 × 26cm
[10½ × 10½in]
•
writing paper for hearts
•
silver thread
•
rubber stamp and inkpad
•
rubber stamp and embossing kit
[optional]
•
red sealing wax, taper and bowl of
water
•
needle and thread
•
decorative edge scissors
•
fabric/paper glue

METHOD

1 Fold the blue card in half and draw a heart so that the top touches the fold. Using decorative edge scissors, cut the two hearts out through the two layers of card, so that they are still joined together at the top.

2 Cut out the hearts from the writing paper in the same way and the same size as those from the blue card – each cut makes two pages, so the number you cut out depends on the number of hearts you want in the book.

3 Lay the folded paper hearts inside the heart-shaped cover and stitch the sheets to the cover where the hearts join at the top. If you do this very slightly behind the fold you will not be able to see the stitches from the front. The paper hearts need not be registered exactly under the cover, as any visible edges will make an interesting effect. Make a small hole near the bottom of the heart cover, pass the silver thread through and make a loop.

4 If you wish, you can decorate the cover and inside pages with a rubber stamp. The hearts on this card have been embossed using an embossing kit (see page 45). Glue the heart notebook to the card mount.

5 After everyone has filled in a page of the card, mask the card with spare paper. Stand a taper in a jar and cover your work surface. Light the taper. Hold the thread and heart with one hand so that the thread is stretched taut on to the card mount to one side of the heart. Hold the stick of sealing wax in the other hand and heat the end in the flame. As soon as the wax begins to soften – this happens very quickly – press the end of the stick on to the loop. You may have to do this several times. Hold the loop stretched until the sealing wax is dry (about 30 seconds).

6 Make small holes and attach a loop of thread to the top of the mount, so that the card can be hung up or make a stand at the back, (see Stand-up Goose on page 68).

Safety Warning
Be very careful with sealing wax – it gets extremely hot. Take care that the stick of wax does not flare up in the taper flame and have a bowl of water ready to dip it into if necessary. When you buy sealing wax, follow the manufacturer's instructions.

Victorian Silk Heart

~

This card is in the style of a Victorian Valentine and uses lace, scraps and padding for the heart.
See also Paper Lace Valentine, page 107.

METHOD

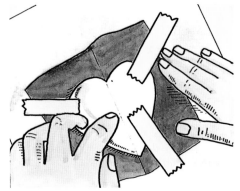

❶ Mark and then cut out a heart-shaped window from the centre of the black card. Cut a similar heart shape from the wadding. Lay the piece of satin over the wadding, and push the satin and wadding gently through the heart window to create a padded effect. Tape this securely in place behind the card.

❹ Glue two pink ribbon bows above and below the heart.

❺ Turn the card over and stick a strip of double-sided tape right around the edge. Stick lengths of lace to this so that they form a frame around the card. Glue the ends of the lace together.

❻ Finally, glue the whole design to the front of the card mount.

❷ Cut out the picture scraps and arrange them around the heart, to the edge of the black card. Allow some to overlap the others. Glue in place.

❸ Cut a length of pink ribbon and a length of lace. Glue the ribbon to the card below the heart, pleating it at the point. Glue the lace on top in the same way, allowing some of the ribbon to show. Cover the ends with two picture scraps.

MATERIALS

Victorian Silk Heart
~

dark red card mount, 35 × 20cm [14 × 8in], scored to fold in middle of long side

•

rectangle of black card approximately 1cm [¹/₂in] smaller all round than front of mount

•

2 sheets Victorian reproduction scraps [available from good stationers or by mail order]

•

1m [1yd] cream lace

•

2 purchased pink satin bows [or make them with thin satin ribbon]

•

cream wide satin ribbon approximately 8 × 8cm [3 × 3in]

•

1m [1yd] pink ribbon

•

wadding or cotton wool

•

scissors

•

double-sided tape

•

PVA glue

MATERIALS

Corrugated Book Card
~

two pieces corrugated cardboard,
22 × 15cm (9 × 6in)
•
handmade floral paper
•
textured paper to contrast with
floral paper
•
postcard
•
fray-check
•
20 × 12.5cm (8 × 5in) tapestried
furnishing fabric
•
suede fabric
•
dried flowers
•
small flat-sided fake pearls
•
decorative buttons or charms
•
narrow satin ribbon
•
gold leaf paint
•
acrylic and stencil paints
•
selection of stencils or rubber
stamps
•
hole punch
•
needle and nylon thread
•
scissors
•
craft knife
•
cutting mat
•
fabric/paper glue

Corrugated Book Card
~

Look for a variation of these fascinating cards in the gallery section on page 115. Uniquely, the four sides of this card are embellished with different but complementary designs. Use the ideas as a wonderful source of inspiration.

METHOD

Front of card

1 Peel the top layer off the corrugated card so that you can decorate the more interesting textured surface beneath. Punch two holes in each of the corrugated pieces of card.

2 Use fray-check on the sides of the tapestry fabric to prevent fraying, following the manufacturer's instructions. Glue to the middle front of the card. Place the postcard on the fabric and glue. Weight with a heavy book to dry flat.

3 Decorate the card by sticking on grass, dried flowers, a tassel and decorative buttons or charms. Reinforce with a few stitches where necessary, using nylon thread.

4 Cover all threads and holes on the rear front by gluing on gift-wrap paper. Paint the edges of the card front with gold leaf paint.

Inside and back of card

5 Cover the greetings page with handmade paper and textured paper. Use an appropriate rubber stamp for your greeting.

6 Turn the card over and stencil a design on to the card using acrylic or stencil paints. When dry, glue on pearls, in accordance with the design.

Assembly

7 Cut 2 strips of suede and ribbon approximately 3mm × 27.5cm (⅛ × 11in). Place the front and back of the card together and thread the strips through the holes, tying loosely, so that the card can easily be opened.

Collected Letters
~

This card was inspired by friendship quilts in which each square is made by friends or family and then joined together. For a special birthday or other occasion, prepare well in advance. Ask friends or family to help you make a card which contains their thoughts and memories of the recipient, and which may be treasured for many years.

METHOD

1 Cut or tear small sheets of watercolour paper, each about 8 × 9cm (3 × 3½in). Tearing gives a more attractive edge: to do this, fold paper sharply and tear along a straight edge or ruler. Send one sheet to each of the friends or family you would like to contribute to the card. Ask them to write a message, make a drawing, copy a poem, include pressed flowers, or leaves, seeds or photographs – anything that reminds them of the person who will receive the card. Both sides of the paper can be used but no objects should be bigger than a quarter of the paper size.

2 When you receive the "letters" back, fold them into four and wrap with tissue, including any flowers, etc. Writing looks interesting when parts of it are seen through the tissue. Do not glue the parcels – simply fold the tissue at the back.

3 Place the parcels on the background paper and cut this to size with decorative-edge scissors; if you don't have these, tear as described in Step 1. Make small holes in the background with a pin at centre top and bottom of each parcel, as close to the parcel as possible – you can mark the points with pencil first.

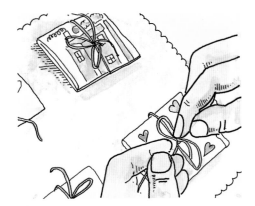

4 Push lengths of the gold thread through the holes from the back of the paper and tie the letter-parcels to the background using double bows.

5 Glue the backing paper to the card mount. The messages can be unwrapped and read, but because the thread is glued to the card under the backing paper it will not slip out through the holes and the letters can be wrapped again and tied back on to the card to keep.

MATERIALS

Collected Letters
~
card mount, 32 × 21cm (13 × 8½in), scored to fold along top centre

•

thick paper or thin card for background

•

textured watercolour paper

•

fine white tissue (available from artists' supply shops)

•

gold thread

•

decorative-edge scissors

•

craft knife

•

cutting mat

•

pin

•

fabric/paper glue

•

pencil

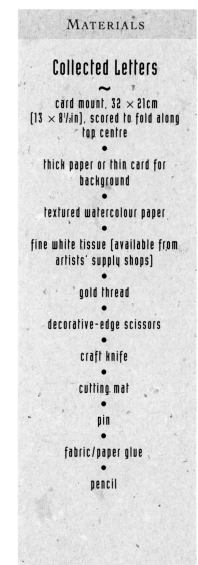

Gallery

1 Key to my Heart

Kate Twelvetrees
An embossed copper heart is wrapped in silk organza, tied with gold thread, then mounted on frayed silk with a hanging, wrapped antique key.

2 Butterflies

Wendy Beardmore
In an even more painstaking variation of the card on page 74, each layer of the butterfly wings being added one at a time with a cocktail stick and a tiny amount of glue.

3 Carnation

Jane Lord
This handmade paper uses real carnation petals, giving a very delicate effect.

4 Peacock/Running Hare/Birds Laying Egg

Julie Morgan
The images on these cards are drawn on to textured backgrounds and then combined with collaged, handmade and painted papers.

5 Heart through a Window

Personal Stamp Exchange
A padded heart within a stamped, embossed decorative border is glimpsed through a cut-out beribboned window mount.

6 Autumn Leaves

Personal Stamp Exchange
Soft, torn tissue edges and colours reflect the embossed, stamped autumn leaves, edged with a twig bound with thin gold wire.

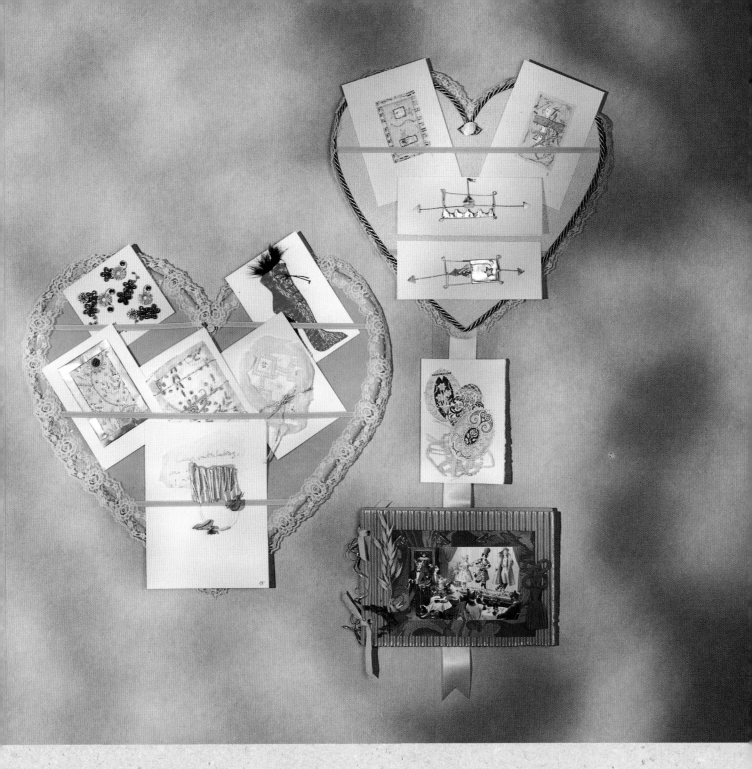

Potpourri Keepsake
~

This card is sealed with ribbon which can be retied after the message has been read. It could then be kept to scent a drawer. Perhaps include a verse from a favourite poem, or write a letter or message using lettering from a book on script to make this more decorative. For a special occasion, perhaps include a small gift inside the card, such as a scented lace handkerchief.

MATERIALS

Potpourri Keepsake
~

thick watercolour paper mount,
28 × 18cm (11 × 7in), scored to
fold along the top of the card and
with deckle edges

•

smaller rectangle of the same
paper

•

pretty handmade paper or deckle-
edged paper, diluted coffee and
gold paint (optional — see Step 3)

•

potpourri, or dried lavender mixed
with dried rose petals

•

dried rosebud

•

fine lace

•

narrow satin ribbon to match roses

•

rubber stamp or stencil (optional —
see Step 5)

•

fabric/paper glue

METHOD

1 Place dried rose petals on the rectangle of paper and cover with lace. Turn the paper and lace over carefully and glue the edges behind, forming a parcel. Alternatively, use the decorative selvage of the lace at the top, in which case don't fold and glue the top edge, but stitch through it with white thread to enclose the petals. Tie the parcel with ribbon, knotting behind.

2 Pierce two holes at the bottom corners of the mount, through both layers. Pass a long piece of ribbon through these holes from the back of the card. Make sure the two ends of ribbon coming through to the front of the card are equal in length. Tie a knot in each of these ends about 8cm (3in) from the edge of the mount.

3 Write a letter or message on pretty paper and glue this inside the card. Alternatively, if you are using a verse, write this out on a piece of deckle-edged paper then stain the paper with diluted coffee to "antique" it, tint with gold paint, and glue it inside the card.

4 After writing the message inside the card, wrap the ribbon back around the edges and tie with a bow in the centre back of the card. The card will stand up after it has been opened, but because the ribbon can't slip out, the card can be resealed.

5 Finally, glue the potpourri parcel to the front of the mount, and perhaps decorate the back of the mount with a rubber stamp or stencilled pattern. Tuck a dried rosebud behind the ribbon.

Cassette Wedding Card
~

Messages of goodwill from the family, a tape of romantic music or something amusing – this is a novelty wedding card that would be fun to make with the children of the family.

METHOD

1 Wrap the cassette case in silver tissue and tie with silver ribbon. Attach to the centre of the mount with the sticky pad.

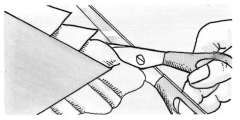

2 Cut strips of silver tissue, pleat and glue around the edge. When dry, cut a wavy pattern along the edges.

3 Apply a wavy line of glue just inside the edge of the mount. Sprinkle with silver glitter and shake off the excess.

4 Cut two small dove shapes from silver card and make holes for their eyes. Decorate the edges with glitter as before.

5 Wrap cake decoration flowers in tissue and tie with ribbon. Glue on bouquets, doves and other cake decorations.

Driftwood Greeting
~

For a completely different type of greeting, experiment with sending your message on other materials, such as this simple piece of driftwood.

METHOD

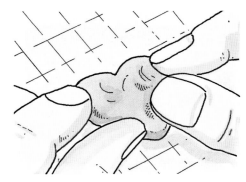

1 Make a small heart from plasticine – either quite flat like a drop of liquid metal, or rounded, as if padded, according to taste. Paint this with PVA to seal. If using polymer or modelling clay, follow manufacturer's instructions carefully.

2 When dry, paint the heart gold. When the paint has dried completely, glue the heart to the driftwood.

3 Tear a piece of paper to the same shape as the back of the driftwood. Write your message on the paper, and bind it to the wood using the gold thread. Alternatively, you can tear a thin strip of paper to fit round the wood, write your message all the way along it, and then fix it round the wood with double-sided tape.

back

front

Take my Heart

~

The list of instructions for this card are only a loose guideline. Experiment with different ways of making hearts, other bought or found objects, wider threads and ribbons, and different-coloured mounts. To achieve the deckle edge on the watercolour, tear it along a sharp edge, such as a metal ruler, or use decorative-edge scissors.

MATERIALS

Take my Heart

~

cream coloured card mount, 30 × 10.5cm (12 × 4¼in), scored to fold in middle

•

watercolour paper, torn to size (see page 13)

•

fine white tissue paper (available from an artists' supply shop)

•

thin copper sheet (available from sculpting supply shops)

•

inexpensive "gold" jewellery heart

•

brooch pin

•

gold cord

•

fine gold thread

•

gold and pink acrylic paint

•

sharp scissors

•

metal file

•

PVA glue

•

all-purpose adhesive

METHOD

1 Cut tiny hearts and a larger one for the brooch from the metal (sharp scissors are adequate for the copper) and file all the edges smooth.

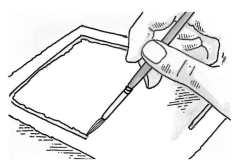

2 Dab or paint small areas of the watercolour paper with gold and pink paint, or paint a "frame" of gold. Tie the paper like a parcel with gold cord, gluing the ends in place just under the edges of the paper.

3 Suspend the bought heart with fine thread from the top of the paper and glue on the tiny hearts.

4 Tear tiny strips of tissue. Apply PVA to these, either with the fingers or a brush, and pleat and stretch them over all the hearts and some parts of the cord. When dry, brush quite dry gold paint over the creases in the tissue, to make it look like fine gold cloth. (The tissue stretched over the jewellery heart binds it to the paper and gives it a more interesting finish.) Glue the paper to the card mount.

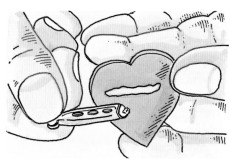

5 Stretch pleated tissue with PVA over the larger copper heart, wrap it behind, and leave to dry. Highlight the tissue pleats with gold paint. Using a strong adhesive, glue the brooch pin to the back of the heart. When this is really dry, pin the brooch over the cord on the card.

Silver Dove Decoration
~

You can buy thin sheet aluminium at a sculptor's supply shop. If you can't find any, use cardboard painted gold or silver, or metallic card. The soft, hand-made paper used for the background gives an interesting edge when torn.

METHOD

❶ Draw or trace the shape for the decoration – star, crown, dove, etc. Cut this from the aluminium using scissors. Also cut out two small stars and file all edges smooth.

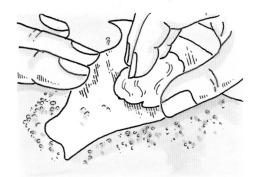

❷ Sprinkle some sand on a work surface and lay the decoration on top. Rub the decoration with tissue or cotton wool, pressing it against the grains of sand to achieve an embossed effect. Emboss lines on the backs of the small stars. Using the point of a used biro, emboss a raised spot for the bird's eye.

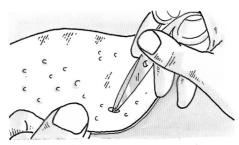

❸ Make a small hole at the top of the bird. Thread silver thread through this, and tie it in a loop.

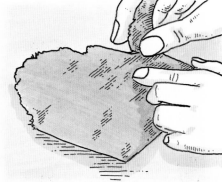

❹ Tear an egg-like shape from the blue paper and glue this to the mount. Fingerprint or stipple gold paint on to the blue background. Fix the two small stars to the paper with double-sided tape.

❺ Finally hang the decoration over the front of the mount and fix it inside the card, using magic tape so that it can be removed easily for future use.

MATERIALS

Silver Dove Decoration
~
card mount, 21 × 14.5cm
[8½ × 5¾in], scored to fold in
middle
•
soft, dark blue handmade paper
•
tissue or piece of cotton wool
•
sheet aluminium
•
sand
•
silver thread
•
gold acrylic paint
•
used biro
•
double-sided tape
•
magic tape
•
scissors
•
metal file
•
cutting mat
•
fabric/paper glue

Basic Quilling
~

For quilling you may use either a needle tool or a slotted tool. The needle tool makes a smaller centre in the rolls and so makes a more attractive design. The slotted tool is easier to use because the slot catches and holds the paper, but it leaves a bend in the paper. The proper weight quilling paper is most important; it rolls smoothly, opens evenly, and holds its shape well. The standard width paper is 3mm (⅛in). Make the board by wrapping waxed paper around a piece of corrugated cardboard.

OTHER MATERIALS

quilling board (see right)
•
tweezers
•
straight pins
•
ruler
•
scissors
•
clear-drying PVA glue

Quilling: To practise, tear off a strip of quilling paper of the length specified in the instructions. To roll with the needle tool, slightly moisten one end of the paper and place that end against the end of your index finger. Position the quilling tool on the end of the paper and press the paper around the tool with your thumb. Roll the paper around the tool with your thumb, keeping the edges as even as possible. Remove the paper from the tool and glue the loose end. When you are first learning, roll each strip in the centre of the needle. After you have become proficient, you may want to use the needle's tip instead. It will leave a smaller hole in the roll's centre.

BASIC SHAPES

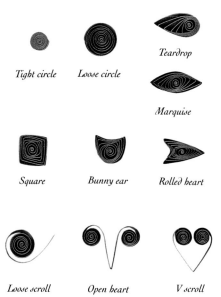

Tight circle   Loose circle   Teardrop

Marquise

Square   Bunny ear   Rolled heart

Loose scroll   Open heart   V scroll

Quilling shapes: The following rolls and scrolls are used in these two designs.
Tight circle: Roll, slide the roll off the tool and glue the loose end closed.
Loose circle: Roll. Slide off tool and allow the coils to expand. Glue the loose end.
Teardrop: Roll a loose circle and pinch a point on one side.
Marquise: Roll a loose circle and pinch on opposite sides.
Square: Make a marquise. Turn it 90 degrees and pinch it again.
Bunny ear: Roll a loose circle. Make a rounded indentation on one side.
Rolled heart: Make a loose circle. Pinch a point on one side. Then make a sharp indentation on the opposite side. Be sure all three points are very sharp.
Loose scroll: Roll one end of the strip, leaving the other end loose.
Open heart: Crease a length of paper in the centre. Roll each end in toward the crease.
V scroll: Crease a length of paper at its centre. Roll each end toward the outside.

METHOD

1 Draw your pattern on a separate piece of paper. Roll the quilling paper with the slotted tool by threading paper into the slot of the tool. Slide the tool to near the strip's end and turn it in a circular motion, keeping the edges even.

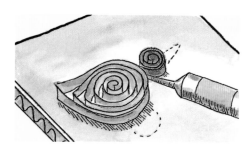

2 Slip your pattern under the waxed paper on the quilling board and pin the first roll directly over the pattern. Use a small amount of glue to attach the second roll to the first.

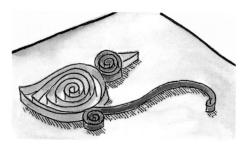

3 Continue adding rolls, using pins to secure until the glue is dry, as needed. Remove the pins and gently lift the design from the waxed paper. Attach to mount with PVA glue, as in the designs shown.

Welcome to the World
~

Balloons: Three 30.5cm (12in) teardrops, three 7.5cm (3in) rolled hearts for knots and three short lengths of paper for string.

Ball: Glue a deep blue 61cm (24in) length, a pale pink 30.5cm (12in) length and a 30.5cm (12in) deep blue length together end to end. Roll into a tight circle beginning with the deep blue 61cm (24in) length. Gently push the centre out to make a conical roll and then spread a thin layer of glue on the inner surface to help it retain its shape.

Sailboat: 20cm (8in) irregular shape (for hull), five 5cm (2in) tight circles for mast, sail cut from white paper.

Kite: Background diamond cut from deep blue paper, 7.5cm (3in) white open heart glued into an 8.2cm (3¼in) V scroll; 10cm (4in) white open heart glued into a 10.8cm (4¼in) V scroll; six 5cm (2in) coloured teardrops; short length of white paper across width of kite; short length of deep blue paper for the tail.

Teddy bear: 61cm (24in) loose circle (body), two 7.5cm (3in) teardrops (arms), two 15cm (6in) loose circles (feet), 30.5cm (12in) loose circle (head), two 5cm (2in) bunny ears (ears), two 2.5cm (1in) tight circles (eyes), 5cm (2in) tight circle (nose). Add a small yellow bow.

Blocks: Use 6mm-wide (⅜in) paper to make three 7.5cm (3in) red, yellow and blue squares. Print a letter on each square.

Duck: 38cm (15in) shaped yellow teardrop for body, 7.5cm (3in) loose circle for head, two 7.5cm (3in) tight circles for feet; length of beige paper for making triangular beak and string.

Quilled Wedding Card
~

Butterfly: Cut a 10 × 2cm (4 × 1in) triangle and roll into a bead beginning with the wide end of triangle. Each wing is a 15cm (6in) and a 10cm (4in) teardrop (standard width) glued together. Wrap a length of gold quill trim around each teardrop.

Flowers: Make four soft ivory flowers using 10cm (4in) bunny ears, two flowers using 7.5cm (3in) bunny ears and three flowers using 5cm (2in) bunny ears.

Flower centres: Glue soft ivory to soft green and roll into a tight circle beginning the roll with the soft ivory. For each large flower use 6.4cm (2½in) soft ivory and 1.3cm (½in) soft green. The medium flowers use 5cm (2in) soft ivory and 1.3cm (½in) soft green, the small flowers use 4cm (1½in) soft ivory and 1.3cm (½in) soft green.

Leaves: Cut six leaves from 1cm (⅜in) width green paper and six leaves from 1cm (⅜in) width gold quill trim.

Scrolls: 2.5cm (1in) and 5cm (1in) pale green loose scrolls.

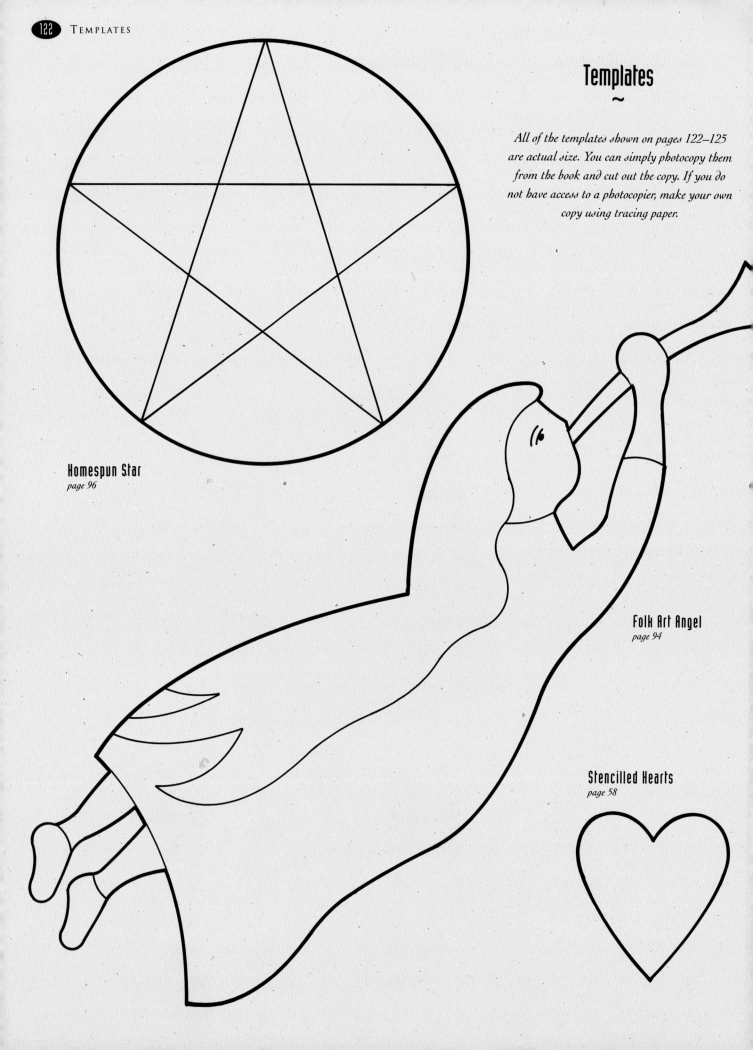

Templates
~

All of the templates shown on pages 122–125 are actual size. You can simply photocopy them from the book and cut out the copy. If you do not have access to a photocopier, make your own copy using tracing paper.

Homespun Star
page 96

Folk Art Angel
page 94

Stencilled Hearts
page 58

Calico Cat
page 93

Stencil Sunface
page 60

Silkscreen Card
page 50

Hand and Heart
page 38

Classic Vase
page 63

Stand-up Goose
page 68

Templates
~

Cross-stitch Heart
page 103

3-D Star *Reduced by 50 per cent*
page 69

Stand-up Pig
page 69

Index

Card Makers

~

Quarto would like to thank all the cardmakers who have kindly allowed us to include their cards in this book.

Special thanks to the following agents for their help and interest: **Elka de Wit** at The Elk, 67 Brighton Road, London N16 8EQ (tel. (0171) 249 9181), representing cardmakers **Thérèse McDermott, Julie Morgan, Judy Pickering,** and **Alana Pryce**; and **Jain Suckling** at **Funky Eclectica,** 12 First Avenue, London W10 4NL (tel. (0181) 964 9411), representing **Irene Baron, Judy Caplin, Cluck, Susan Codmer, Jan Cooper, Julie Dean, Ingrid**

Duffy, Hand and Heart Design, Susan Luqman, Mayhem Designs, Rosalind Miller, Helen rowan, Sands, Penny Saxby, Sparkle Designs and Sophie Williams. Kate Twelvetrees' cards are distributed in the US by **The English Card Company** (tel. (516) 627 3011), or she can be contacted at her London studio on (0181) 809 1593. **Vinci Draper** at **The English Card Company,** 14c Hargrave Park, London N19 5JL, also distributes cards by **Sarah Jane Brown, Jilly Marcuson,** and **Sally Norris.**

Andrea Liss can be contacted at **Hannah Handmade Cards,** Evanston, Illinois; **Malinda Johnston** is at the L:ake City Craft Co, Nixa, Montana. **The Crescent Cardboard Company** are based in Wheeling, Illinois; Paper Troupe are in Bensenville, Illinois; and the **Personal Stamp Exchange** are in Petaluma, California.

All other cardmakers can be contacted care of Quarto Publishing.

Quarto would also like to thank Amazing Grates, 61–63 High Road, East Finchley, London N2 8AB for supplying mantelpieces for photography.

Project Makers

~

Kate Twelvetrees 20, 24, 25, 26, 27 (right), 28, 29, 30, 31, 36, 40, 41, 49, 51, 53 (left), 56 (right), 57, 73 (right), 96 (right), 107 (left), 108, 109, 110, 113, 116, 117 (right), 118, 119

Lucinda Ganderton 38, 39 (left and right), 60 (right), 68, 88, 93, 94, 96 (left), 103 (right), 106, 107 (right)

Fenella Brown 21 (left), 23, 34, 46, 62, 63, 72, 89, 90, 91, 92, 95 (left and right), 97, 100, 102, 111, 117 (left)

Mary Fellows 21 (right), 22, 35, 47, 48, 58, 59

Elaine Hill 27 (left), 53 (right), 60 (left), 61, 66, 67, 69 (right), 81, 84

Melanie Brasch 69 (left), 70, 71, 73 (left), 76, 77, 78, 79, 83 (left and right), 85, 103 (left)

Clare Baggaley and Sally Bond 82

Cari Haysom 52, 56 (left), 57 (left)

Bobbie Hamburg 112

Tushar Parekh 37 (left and right)

Rachel Purser 80

Malinda Johnstone 120, 121

Michelle Powell 44, 45

Sarbjit Natt 50, 101